M000305489

THE WEIR GROUP

THE WEIR GROUP

The history of a Scottish engineering legend, 1872–2008

William Weir

P

PROFILE BOOKS

First published in Great Britain in 2008 by
Profile Books Ltd
3A Exmouth House
Pine Street
Exmouth Market
London EC1R 0JH
www.profilebooks.com

10 9 8 7 6 5 4 3 2 1

A CIP catalogue record for this book is available from the British Library.

ISBN 978 1 86197 886 8

Typeset in Bembo by MacGuru
info@macguru.org.uk

Printed and bound in Great Britain by
Clays, Bungay, Suffolk

The paper this book is printed on is certified by the © 1996 Forest Stewardship
Council A.C. (FSC). It is ancient-forest friendly. The printer holds FSC chain of
custody SGS-COC-2061

Contents

Illustrations

Hydraulic power pumps at the Beatrix gold mine in
    South Africa.
Concentrated sulphuric acid pump by Lewis Pumps.
EnviroTech scrubber pump for flue gas desulphurisation.
Zeron™ alloy fittings.
Boiler feed pump assembly at Cathcart.
Downhole gas/liquid handling pump for Texaco.
Desalination plant at Jebel Ali, Dubai.
Hopkinson subsea ball valves.
The Catton's AOD (argon oxygen decarburisation)
    furnace.
A Warman 650HTP pump by Weir Minerals South
    America being installed in Chile in early 2008
Atwood and Morrill 96-inch stainless steel Tricentric
    valve.

Acknowledgements

There are many people whom I must thank for their contribution to writing this volume. Paul Forty of Profile Books has been so helpful, cheerful and friendly as my editor, and showed exemplary patience at my delays in completing it. I must acknowledge the assistance I have had from W. J. Reader's earlier history of the Weir Group, which covered the period up to 1970 and greatly helped me by providing a framework of the events of those years. Ian Boyd, formerly finance director of Weir's, provided valuable material and comments, as did Duncan MacLeod, a former director, and John Hood of Weir Pumps. Helen Walker of the Weir Group and Alan Mitchelson helped me in the same way. My secretary, Isabel Grieve, typed up the text and patiently endured my frequent alterations and rewriting. My wife, Marina, put up with my frequent bad moods. So many thanks to all of these. Finally, I must thank my late grandfather, the 1st Lord Weir. I lived with him for two years when he was in his 80s, and he told me much about the early and exciting days of the firm.

Foreword

The Weir Group was founded in 1872 by George and James Weir, whose grandmother was a descendant of Scotland's national bard, Robert Burns.

This was the time when sailing ships were starting to give way to steam, and the foundations of the business were laid by the inventions of James Weir in dealing with the technical challenges of steam propulsion.

Today the Weir Group is a global company with more than 9,000 employees operating in over 50 countries. Although most of the Group's profit is now generated from outside Scotland, its headquarters remain in Glasgow.

This book has been written by William, Viscount Weir, who is the great grandson of James Weir and who spent his working life with the Group. It is not a compilation of statistics, but rather a very human tale with its share of dramas. William takes a very honest and candid look at the successes – and at one point near-extinction – of the company and at the personalities involved.

The focus of the book is from 1954, when the author joined the business. William was educated in Canada and at Eton before going to Trinity College, Cambridge, where he was an exhibition scholar and gained a blue for golf. He is a natural storyteller and raconteur, and this book not only provides an insight into the evolution of the Weir Group, but is also a fascinating read.

The Lord Smith of Kelvin Kt
Chairman, The Weir Group PLC

Weir family tree

Principal members of the Weir family

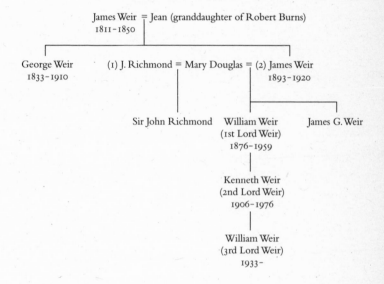

James Weir = Jean (granddaughter of Robert Burns)
1811–1850

George Weir
1833–1910

(1) J. Richmond = Mary Douglas = (2) James Weir
1893–1920

Sir John Richmond

William Weir
(1st Lord Weir)
1876–1959

James G. Weir

Kenneth Weir
(2nd Lord Weir)
1906–1976

William Weir
(3rd Lord Weir)
1933–

Chronology of key events

1872 George and James Weir form partnership of G. & J. Weir in Liverpool and move to Glasgow in 1873.

1881 The famous direct-acting pump is patented.

1884 First land-based desalination plant built at Safaga in Egypt.

1886 Factory built at Holm Foundry, Cathcart.

1895 G. & J. Weir incorporated as company. James Weir buys out George Weir.

1902 William Weir (later 1st Lord Weir) becomes managing director at age of 26.

1906 HMS *Dreadnought* built, precipitating naval arms race.

1912 Uniflo condenser introduced. Pipeline built for Anglo Persian oil company.

1915 William Weir joins Lloyd George's Ministry of Munitions.

1918 William Weir created Lord Weir; joins War Cabinet as Secretary of State for Air.

1919 51% of Drysdale's (centrifugal pumpmakers) acquired.

1921 Argus foundry constructed.

1924 Cardonald factory established to produce steel houses.
      Zenith works established to produce Monel metal.

1926 Investment made in Cierva Autogiro Company.

1945 Balance of 49% of Drysdale's acquired.

1946   G. & J. Weir becomes public listed company.
Weir Housing Corporation formed.

1951   Weir Valves formed.

1955   Lord Weir and Sir John Richmond retire. Kenneth
Weir (later 2nd Lord Weir) becomes chairman.

1956   William Simons (shipbuilders) acquired. Merged
with Lobnitz in 1959.

1957   Control of Peacock Brothers in Canada acquired.

1958   First multiflash desalination plant built, in Guernsey.
Investment in Catton and Co. (steel foundry): 100%
acquired in 1960.

1959   ITAM (Société d'Installation Thermique et
Auxiliaire des Machines) in France acquired. Later
to become Weiritam and then Delas Weir.
G. & J. Weir Holdings formed. Outside directors
join board.
1st Lord Weir dies.

1961   Interest in aircraft equipment acquired through
purchase of C. F. Taylor.
Simons-Lobnitz sold to Alexander Stephen.

1962   Weir Westgarth formed: 50/50 venture with
Richardsons Westgarth.

1956   Jopling steel foundry acquired.

1967   Company renamed The Weir Group.

1969   Osborn Hadfield Steel Founders acquired.
Harland Engineering acquired after hostile
takeover. Merged with G. & J. Weir to form Weir
Pumps Ltd.
Agreement with Studebaker-Worthington: Weir's
acquire 50% of Worthington Simpson.

1970   New foundry for Catton's started.

1972   William Weir (later 3rd Lord Weir) becomes
chairman.

1974   Majority share of Weir Construction sold.

1976   Former Drysdale's plant at Yoker closed.
        2nd Lord Weir dies.

1978   C. F. Taylor companies (Aircraft Equipment
        division) sold.
        Livorno factory for Polypac SpA built.

1980   Weir Pacific Valves and Osborn Hadfield and Alston
        foundries closed.
        Heavy losses lead to financial crisis and many
        redundancies.

1981   Financial reconstruction: Sir Francis Tombs
        becomes chairman in place of William Weir.
        Further disposals. Recovery in profits. 40% of
        company effectively controlled by interests of Lord
        Rothschild and D. H. Ruttenberg. Ruttenberg
        joins board.

1982   Ronald Garrick becomes chief executive.

1983   William Weir again becomes chairman.

1986   Steel foundries sold to William Cook.
        Shareholding in Delas Weir sold.

1987   Mather and Platt Machinery acquired.

1988   Liquid Gas Equipment acquired.

1989   Hopkinson's acquired.

1990   Rights issue. Strachan and Henshaw, and Atwood
        and Morrill acquired.

1991   Peabody Floway acquired.

1992   Darchem acquired.

1994   Rights issue to purchase EnviroTech.

1997   Management of Devonport Royal Dockyard taken
        on with partners Halliburton and BICC.

1999   William Weir retires. Sir Ronald Garrick becomes
        chairman.
        Warman International acquired.

2000   Darchem sold.

2001   Mark Selway becomes chief executive.

2002   Sir Ronald Garrick retires. Sir Robert Smith (later Lord Smith) becomes chairman.

2005   Gabbioneta in Italy acquired. Hopkinson's relocated. Desalination business sold.

2007   Sale of Weir Pumps' Cathcart operations and Cathcart site.
Devonport business sold.
Acquisition of SPM Flow Control of Fort Worth, Texas, and of Multiflo of Queensland, Australia.

2008   Acquisition of C. H. Warman of South Africa; Mesa Manufacturing Inc., of Odessa, Texas; and Standard Oilfield Services Limited of Baku, Azerbaijan.

1

Early days

1872–1918

By the last quarter of the nineteenth century, the West of Scotland was firmly established as not only a great manufacturing centre, but also one which was still expanding. As sail gave way to steam, shipbuilding on the Clyde gained the pre-eminent position in the world. On the demand side it was supported by the strong position of British ship owners, and on the supply side by a vigorous local iron and steel industry, based on the coal fields of Lanarkshire and Ayrshire, and which was to include such famous names as William Baird, Stewarts and Lloyds, Colvilles and William Beardmore. There were numerous other heavy engineering enterprises associated in some cases with shipbuilding, but often involved in other markets. One example was Babcock & Wilcox, the boilermakers, based in Renfrew, but of American parentage, later to be joined by Yarrow's, who emigrated from the Thames to the Clyde and brought with them a combination of boilermaking and fast warship construction. Other prominent engineering concerns were Sir William Arrol, in structural iron and steel, who built the Forth Railway Bridge; Glenfield and Kennedy, in waterworks engineering; and the steam locomotive builders who subsequently became North British Locomotive. On a smaller scale were those companies who provided specialist equipment, often to the shipbuilding industry. Well-known names included Bull's, who made propellers; Hasties, who made steering gear; and Dewrance, who made valves; together with a host of others.

Industrial activity was in no sense confined to shipbuilding and other, often associated heavy engineering concerns. Light engineering was epitomised by Singer's huge sewing machine works. They were one of the first American companies to become truly international, as its proprietor emphasised by calling his sons Paris, Washington and Frankfurt. Fortunately, one may say, he did not have a fourth son who might have struggled under the name Clydebank Singer. Textiles were another major industry, in which J. & P. Coats virtually controlled the world's thread manufacture. Indeed, at the start of the twentieth century Coats were one of the five largest quoted firms in the world. Carpet making was represented by, among others, the ancient and quaintly named United Turkey Red Co. In chemicals, Charles Tennant was a famous name, and the giant chimney over their works, nicknamed Tennant's Lum, or Tennant's Stalk, was a notable landmark in Glasgow.

The West of Scotland was therefore home at that time, and for a considerable period thereafter, to numerous manufacturing companies who were not only successful in local terms, but were also often leaders in their particular field in the United Kingdom and even internationally. This state of affairs generally endured up to the start of the First World War. There were subsequent casualties during the inter-war Great Depression. Even so, as late as the end of the Second World War, many of these firms were still alive and well. In spite of all the problems the Depression caused there were high growth industries in the United Kingdom during that period, notably the electrical and automotive sector, but Scotland did not share in these to any significant extent.

Sadly, however, not one of the well-known names of that time still survives. It is true that some parts of those once large companies still exist, but in virtually every case they are now subsidiaries of much larger enterprises, whether based in the UK or overseas. Certainly none of them exists in an independent form, based in Scotland and with their headquarters still there. Of course, their places have been taken by newer industries, but all too often simply in the form of branch factories.

The one exception to this dismal tale is the Weir Group. This book recounts the Group's history over some 130 years, although it concentrates mainly on the period since 1954. During most of that latter time I worked for the company, for many years in a senior position. I therefore also attempt to explain the unique survival of the firm, which involves discussing the reasons why various strategic decisions were made, the reasons for failure and success, and the character and interaction of the main personalities involved.

The Weir Group started life in 1872 as G. & J. Weir, a partnership between two brothers, George and James Weir, both marine engineers. To put that year into a historical context, we should recall that veterans of Waterloo were then still alive, as were also a tiny handful of those who had fought at Trafalgar as midshipmen or ship's boys, when little more than children. The Crimean War and the Indian Mutiny were quite recent events. No railway or road yet crossed North America. On a more trivial scale, the first soccer match between England and Scotland took place that year. (It was a goalless draw, by the way.) In England

the FA Cup Final was won in the 1870s by the Old Eto-
nians, who beat Blackburn Rovers because, as the press put
it, 'they ran faster'. And on a macabre note, the last public
hanging in Britain had taken place in Glasgow only seven
years earlier, and the last outbreak of cholera in the city was
recent history. More relevant to this history of Weir's was
the fact that, although the bulk of the world's shipping was
still carried by sail – and indeed the finest sailing ship ever,
the clipper *Cutty Sark*, was built by Denny's in Dumbarton
in 1869 – sail was rapidly giving way to steam, and the
Clyde was becoming the predominant shipbuilding centre
of the world.

Glasgow was also the home of important ship owners,
and this was to be of great benefit to Weir's. Famous lines,
then and afterwards, included Maclay and Macintyre –
known to its crews as 'muck and misery' – and the Hogarth
line from Ardrossan in Ayrshire – known as 'the hungry
Hogarth's'. Of both of these lines it was said that no seagulls
followed their ships, such was the paucity of their victuals.
Other famous names included Andrew Weir's Bank Line.
Their owner, later Lord Inverforth, reputedly had a great
dislike of expenditure on paint. He used to observe his
ships leaving and coming into Glasgow through a large
telescope. Accordingly his superintendent painted only the
starboard side of a ship when it was in its home port, so that
his Lordship could not see the new paint when it went
down river. Once down the coast and out of sight, they
stopped and the crew painted the port side.

The Allan Line was another Glasgow name, and it subsequently became the basis of Canadian Pacific Steamships.
The Anchor Line and Cayzer-Irvine (the Clan Line), much
later called British and Commonwealth, were other notable
names. The Andersons from Orkney founded the Peninsu-
lar and Oriental (P&O) Line. Two of the most

entrepreneurial owners of all were Sir William Burrell and his brother. They regularly sold ships and reordered to take the benefit of technical developments and thus of more economic vessels. They were very close to Weir's, and they judged the shipping cycle brilliantly. Sir William's great memorial today is the Burrell Collection in Glasgow, which reflected a taste and shrewdness as a collector that was the equal of his commercial abilities. Although very rich, he was, like many of his countrymen, pretty frugal, and known to take porridge for lunch at Claridge's Hotel when in London. The superintendent engineers of the lines were important customers, often in the mould of Kipling's MacAndrew, and were frequent visitors to Weir's. Many still chewed tobacco and accordingly there was a polished copper spittoon and a whisky decanter on the boardroom table. Both were still there in the 1950s, although the former had fortunately ceased to be used by that time.

For Scots, both at home and abroad, whether as expatriates or emigrants, this period saw the flowering of the Protestant work ethic. Great fortunes and commercial empires were built, often by men who had risen by spirit and ability from modest beginnings. The predominant names in iron, steel, and coal have already been mentioned, as have those in textiles. The great Clyde shipbuilders included Scott's, Stephen's, Lithgow's, John Elder and John Brown. In the financial world, two developments by Scots were noteworthy. Robert Fleming invented the investment trust, and a minister of the kirk in Dumfries founded the Trustee Savings Bank. In the East of Scotland, jute and linoleum industries flourished, and Glasgow was home not only to merchant houses like James Finlay and MacKinnon and Mackenzie, but also to the Burmah Oil Company.

Overseas, Scottish emigrants flourished. Of many, it is enough to mention just two, both of whom started their careers with little or nothing. Andrew Carnegie built, with his partner Henry Frick, Carnegie Steel, which, after the merger engineered by J. P. Morgan at the turn of the century, became US Steel. Important as Carnegie's industrial contribution was, it was dwarfed by his charitable legacy, which established a tradition for the rich in the USA which endures to this day, to the immense benefit of educational, medical and research institutions. And in Canada, Donald Smith, an emigrant from Craigellachie, who joined the Hudson's Bay Company at the age of sixteen and was still at its head when he died at 96 as Lord Strathcona, at that time also effectively controlled the Canadian Pacific Railway and the Bank of Montreal. He was an emblem of Scottish success and indeed also of good works. Queen Victoria once said that he was the best man in her Empire.

As well as the Scots emigrants, there were the Scots expatriates. Perhaps the most famous was the firm of Jardine Matheson, which happily endures to this day. From their beginnings (not considered very fashionable today) as opium traders, they built a great trading house in the Far East. Equally notable in the East was James Mackay, who subsequently became Lord Inchcape and not only founded Inchcape, a great trading house, but also gained control of the P&O Line. Another Scot, largely forgotten today, was David Cargill, the founder of Burmah Oil. Burmah financed the Anglo Persian Oil Company, which later became British Petroleum, and they still held 25 per cent of it until the Iranian Revolution and the overthrow of the Shah in the late 1970s, when they almost became bankrupt and had to sell the shareholding.

This account of the activities of Scots in that period may seem a digression from a history of a particular Glasgow firm. It is nothing of the sort, however. It is important because the spirit and attitude of such people was an important part of the background against which the firm was founded and the Weir brothers worked. Although Weir's never became anything like as large as some of these other heroic enterprises, the spirit and outlook of James and George Weir and of James's sons were not at all different from those of the founders and proprietors of those companies whose success was a continuing example to them.

Social historians have of course remarked that although, in this period of what might be described as unrestrained capitalism (that is, from the mid nineteenth century until Lloyd George's People's Budget of 1909), the owners of industry may have benefited greatly, their workforces certainly did not correspondingly prosper, despite the efforts of an increasingly strong trades union movement. Unfortunately, trades union efforts in those days, instead of concentrating on higher wages or a greater share of success and profits, often tended towards a kind of Luddite protectionism of established working practices and a resistance to change. Later in Weir's history it was this which conditioned the strongly adversarial posture towards the trades unions held by William Weir, James Weir's elder son, during the long period when he was the head of the company. This situation was in marked contrast to that in the USA, where Henry Ford, although he could certainly afford to pay high wages from his immense profits and outstanding productivity, positively favoured doing so because it would increase the number of customers for his products. Apart from this astuteness, however, he was described in the memoirs of one of his chief lieutenants as having 'a loaded ignorance and prejudice on almost every subject'.

The father of George and James Weir was born in humble circumstances and was for some time a coal miner, or collier. He was certainly fortunate not to be an 'indentured collier'.

This awful practice, which persisted until early in the nineteenth century, was very close to slavery. Indentured colliers
had to wear iron collars bearing the name of the coal owner
to whom they 'belonged'. He was however very poorly paid
indeed. His grandson (my own grandfather) told me that at
one time his grandfather had only been paid 5 shillings a
week. When he walked home from work one day he had
dropped one of the two half crowns that made up his pay, so
he rose at dawn and walked slowly back until, by great good
luck, he found it. Hard times produce hard men.

Hard practices long continued in coal mining. In the
1960s, an old retired miner recounted in a letter to the
Ayrshire Post that even in the 1930s at the Annbank pit
groups of miners still bid against each other to cut coal at
a face for the lowest cost. No wonder that Keir Hardie
became one of the earliest Labour MPs for the Cumnock
area in Ayrshire, or that Willie Gallacher became Communist MP for a mining area in Fife, or perhaps that Arthur
Scargill became such a force in his own time. The Weir
brothers clearly came from the toughest of backgrounds.
Their father died when quite young, and the brothers owed
much to their mother, Jean, a woman of great character and
determination. She was a granddaughter of Robert Burns,
descended from his first child, Bess, who was the illegiti-
mate daughter of the poet by Elizabeth Paton, a farm
servant from Mauchline in Ayrshire. Bess was the subject of
two of Burns's most moving poems, and he would have
married her mother if it had not been for the opposition
of his brother Gilbert, who considered her socially
inferior.

Jean Weir was anxious for her sons to succeed in the
world. She therefore wanted them to have good appren-
ticeships, and in order to pay for them, she took in sewing
and embroidery work. James Weir mainly served his time

with the firm of the noted engineer and shipbuilder John Elder, whose company Randolph and Elder eventually became the Fairfield Shipbuilding and Engineering Company of Govan. Those days saw the beginning of the great age of steam power at sea, and James Weir was fortunate to be trained in a company which was in the forefront of technical progress. Elder, in particular, was a pioneer in the development of the compound steam engine. By using the steam at decreasing pressures and consecutively in separate cylinders (as in the triple-expansion engine), not only did this greatly improve the efficiency and economy of steam propulsion, but it also brought with it a number of technical challenges. It was finding successful solutions to these that was to become the basis of G. & J. Weir's business for many years.

James Weir, although the younger brother of George, was very much the dominant figure once G. & J. Weir was formed. As an apprentice he had showed early evidence of a remarkable talent, and had even designed a governor (a device which regulated engine speed) and been given time off by his employers to develop it. After his apprenticeship he went to sea and served as an engineer on the SS *Arabian*, belonging to the Bibby Line of Liverpool, from 1865 to 1870, winning his Board of Trade ticket as a first class engineer in 1868. During this period he devoted much time to studying the problems of steam ship machinery and developing ideas for solutions to them. He left the sea in 1871, and he and his brother George set themselves up as marine engineering consultants, first in Liverpool and then, from 1874 onwards, in Glasgow.

James Weir's first patent was for the Hydrokineter, a device to improve circulation in boilers, thus enabling ships to raise steam more quickly. He followed this with a stream of other designs. G. & J. Weir's first manufacturing order was for a pair of boiler feed pumps for the Clyde Shipping Company, who until very recently operated tugs on the River Clyde. Originally the brothers had no workshops and had to subcontract manufacture, and it was the need to manufacture more effectively which led them to take the decision in 1886 to buy land at Cathcart from the Stirling Maxwell estate and set up on it a machine shop, brass foundry and smithy. Their idea was to have a factory in pleasant countryside surroundings, but Glasgow expanded more quickly than they could have foreseen.

This was a period of rapid growth in the building of steam ships, particularly on the Clyde. In 1880, for example, 436 steam ships with a total of 340,000 tons were launched in the UK. By 1889, this had grown to 558 ships with a total of 553,000 tons, most of them being built on the Clyde. At the same time, technical developments led to a rapid rate of obsolescence, as one generation of design succeeded another. It was the challenges that resulted from the vastly increased use of steam power that gave the brothers their opportunity, and it was their success in meeting them that drove the success of G. & J. Weir.

Clearly the economics of steam versus sail depended greatly on improving the efficiency of the boiler and engine so that the amount of coal consumed could be minimised. This reduced the expenditure on fuel, increased the range between stops for refuelling, and maximised the amount of cargo that could be carried. To achieve this required higher pressure boilers, so that the engine could do more work. That, however, meant that a very reliable pump was needed to feed the water to the boiler at such pressures, particularly when the water-tube boiler was introduced. Previously the boiler-feed pumps had simply worked off the main engines. James Weir therefore developed the independent direct-acting steam-driven reciprocating pump, the key feature of which was its piston-valve chest, which controlled the flow of steam to it. This was a most elegant piece of design, of considerable complexity and ingenuity, but of great reliability. No competitor ever equalled the Weir direct-acting pump. It remained in use for decades by land and sea, and its characteristic sound of wheeze followed by clunk was familiar to generations of engineers around the world. If it ever stopped working the remedy was often a simple one. In the words of Miss North, for many years secretary in the company's London office, to a user who rang for advice, 'Just strike it smartly with a hammer, sir.' Indeed for years the pumps were sent out with an appropriately sized hammer hanging on a string.

To many users, the pumps, which were almost always sold in pairs – one working, and one standby – were referred to, after the firm's proprietors, as 'Geordie and Jimmy'. At sea, some engineers even led a piece of string from the pump to their cabin with a weight on the end so that they could see from the comfort of their bunk whether the crucial feed pump was going up and down. Sometimes they made complaints, highly personalised, such as 'Geordie's doing fine, but there is a wee bit of trouble with Jimmy.'

The next problem was to obtain more useful work from the steam, and hence greater efficiency and better fuel consumption, together with reduced boiler corrosion. The development of the triple expansion engine made it possible to bleed off some of the steam after it had expanded in the high pressure and intermediate pressure cylinders and use it not only to heat the feed water on its way back from the condenser to the boiler but also to avoid corrosion by removing air from the feed water. James Weir designed and patented such a system and thus was the originator of the closed feed heating system which is still today a fundamental element in thermal power stations. This was a major advance in applied thermodynamics, the subject to which James Weir applied himself throughout his life.

A further problem was that of water supply. The higher pressure boilers required water to make up for losses due to leakage, but to avoid corrosion and scaling it needed to be water of a higher degree of purity than could often be obtained from public water supplies at ports of call. Moreover, it was necessary to have additional supplies of fresh water for the passengers on liners. To carry sufficient water was expensive and impractical. This problem was solved by the invention of the first practical marine evaporator, which distilled sea water to produce a high purity product. It was not an original idea. Indeed, Benjamin Franklin had proposed such a solution in the eighteenth century, and Lord Napier had used 'sea water boilers' when he invaded Abyssinia earlier in the nineteenth century. James Weir's evaporator was, however, the first really workable and reliable device. It was also the precursor of G. & J. Weir's subsequent development of the first large-scale modern desalination plants on land.

The first land-based plant was built for the Safaga Phosphate Company on the Red Sea in Egypt in 1882. The granddaughter of the plant's manager told me that after the water had been used domestically it was carefully saved and then used to irrigate the vegetables in their garden; an early and admirable example of what today the environmentalist community would call recycling.

These three inventions – the boiler feed pump, the closed feed heating system and the marine evaporator – represented outstanding and innovative solutions to the main technical challenges of steam propulsion, and a quite remarkable contribution by one man to technical advance. Nor were they the only developments the firm made.

Others of significance included air pumps to extract non-condensible gases from the condenser, extraction pumps to remove the condensed steam from the condenser, major design improvements to the condenser itself, and automatic controllers of the flow of water back to the feed pump and hence to the boiler.

The combination of all these devices with an overall understanding of the thermodynamics of the steam cycle enabled Weir's to design and supply as an integrated whole the entire system of equipment from the exhaust of the steam engine back to the boiler itself. From a commercial point of view, this unique ability in system design, combined with the reliability of the individual pieces of equipment, allowed Weir's to charge premium prices for their equipment. For as long as steam was the preferred means of ship propulsion, Weir's therefore enjoyed a uniquely strong position in the industry, and for a considerable period easy market access was reinforced by the dominant position of British shipbuilding and close relationships with the many important British ship owners.

Another highly important factor behind Weir's early and continuing success was that, in addition to the strong position of British ship owners in world trade, Britain was a major naval power. Not only did the requirements of the Royal Navy often serve as a counterbalance when commercial shipbuilding was in recession, but the Royal Navy was also continually seeking and supporting technical advances to improve the range, speed and reliability of its warships. As a result, from the earliest days the relationship with the Royal Navy was so close that Weir's enjoyed a continuous virtual monopoly for the supply of its requirements. Many foreign navies followed where the Royal Navy led.

In the middle part of the nineteenth century, the Royal

Navy had been somewhat neglected. In the 1890s, with the foundation of the Navy League and the impact of Captain Alfred Thayer Mahan's writings on sea power, naval affairs became a matter of strong public and political interest, further stimulated by the German Naval Law of 1898, which started serious naval development by a country which had previously confined itself to the land. The appearance in 1906 of HMS *Dreadnought* made all other battleships obsolete overnight and precipitated a naval armament race. *Dreadnought* was of revolutionary design in her armament, her protective armour and her propulsion. She was built in conditions of great secrecy. At Weir's, only William Weir knew about her, and the machinery that Weir's built for her was ostensibly destined for a mythical power station near Birmingham whose name he had invented.

The success of the business was not, however, simply the result of designing the right equipment. It also depended on high quality manufacture, as some of the products, such as feed pumps, were quite difficult to make. Moreover, the machine tools available in the early days were not always satisfactory. At an early stage, in 1887, C. R. Lang, a member of the family who owned Lang's of Johnstone, a successful manufacturer of lathes, was recruited as a partner. At a time when there were very few academically trained engineers in industry, Charles Lang had studied in London as a Whitworth Scholar. He was to be in charge of production for many years. Charlie Lang was a stern, bearded man with an unbending outlook, of whom his colleagues once said that he only had to raise his eyebrows in the shops to start a strike.

To meet Weir's requirements the machine tool makers G. & A. Harvey built – to Weir's design – the first horizontal boring mills, subsequently to become a standard machine tool in heavy engineering. Among other innovations was the multiple-head milling machine, again built to Weir's design by the Ingersoll company in the USA. Thus the company was from its earliest days a technical leader not only in product design, but also in manufacturing organisation and methods. In 1898 Weir's introduced the premium-bonus system of payment by results, widely known as the Halsey Weir system, whereby the worker and the firm shared any saving from turning out work faster than a pre-determined time allowance.

Much attention was also given to iron foundry practice, and to the use of standardised components which could be used across a wide part of the product range. Training was not neglected either, and sometime around 1900 an apprentice school was established with its own schoolmaster. This was certainly the first school of its kind in Scotland. Not only did Weir's train engineers for itself, but many former Weir's apprentices subsequently joined the shipping lines who were important customers. As an example, young Chinese were being trained in Glasgow from 1900 for the China Merchants Shipping Company, which was owned by the last Empress of China and managed by Tom Weir, the brother of George and James. One of these young men continued to write from China to the chairman of Weir's every year until 1970 to report what was happening in his life.

In 1895, G. & J. Weir turned itself from a partnership into a limited company. The shareholders were mainly the Weirs, with J. D. Latta (a cousin of the family) and C. R. (Charlie) Lang as the others. Shortly afterwards, George Weir was bought out by his brother and left the firm, moving to Australia. He was a highly religious man, and family legend has it that he and James finally fell out when the latter objected to George casting church bells in the foundry free of charge.

Around 1900, James Weir started to pass the day-to-day running of the business to his eldest son, William, who was later to become the 1st Lord Weir. William was appointed managing director in 1902 at the early age of 26, and at the salary, huge for those days, of £25,000 a year. The senior management of the company at that time, apart from him, were Charles Lang in charge of manufacturing; J. D. Latta, who looked after sales; and John Richmond (William Weir's half-brother), who handled administration and finance. In 1909 J. G. (James) Weir, William's younger brother, joined the firm as a director. For most of the next forty years the business was run by this team, apart from Latta, who was to resign in 1917 in protest against the profits the firm was making on wartime aircraft construction, because his sons were at this time pilots in the Royal Flying Corps – a somewhat curious decision, as Weir's had already committed their war profits to good causes, such as the Red Cross.

When James Weir stepped back from direct management of the business, he did not give his shares to his two sons and stepson, John Richmond. Instead, he lent them the money to buy the shares, which they then had to repay to their father over the years. James retired to an estate he bought in Dumfriesshire where – having little confidence in architects – he designed his own house, Over Courance. (Although he was a brilliant design engineer, he was not quite so good at architecture. He omitted to put in stairs to the cook's bedroom, and the poor lady had to ascend at night on a step-ladder through a trap door.) He spent much time travelling. He also wrote a complex book called *The Energy System of Matter*, which explored the thermodynamics of the planet, and he engaged in correspondence with Lord Kelvin on the nature of the universe; a surprising activity in retirement for a man of so very little formal education.

One story from William Weir's early days is worth recounting. By the age of nineteen, he had never been out of Scotland, so his father said he should have some commercial experience, and he was sent to London to see the Thames Iron Works, a shipbuilder on the river who had built a battleship and owed Weir's a lot of money. William duly arrived in the City and went to the Thames Iron Works offices, where a young man, the company secretary, met him. He told William that he could not expect any payment as the company was on the verge of insolvency, and then added the disturbing remark, 'Please, Mr Weir, do not show surprise when you see the chairman.' At this, William was ushered into an imposing boardroom. At the end of a long table, to his utter amazement, was a large iron box, from which an aged gentleman's head protruded. It was the chairman. He suffered from some acute rheumatic complaint and spent much of the day encased in warm mud. You do not find that sort of thing so often in the City these days. Sure enough, the visit produced no payment and the Thames Iron Works went bankrupt. The young man who had met William was Robert Kindersley, later to become Lord Kindersley, the head of Lazards in London, and a lifelong friend.

J. G. Weir deserves special mention as a most unusual and talented man. He was sent to Dollar Academy, Scotland's oldest boarding school, in Clackmannanshire, because there was an outstanding mathematics teacher there, but left when he turned sixteen because they could not teach him anything more. He then had further training at the company's works at Cathcart, and in Germany, both in the Atlas Engineering works and at the technical institute in Freiburg. In due course he was for many years in charge of the technical direction of the company.

He was also a true gentleman, and was so angry when

his sister Mary was jilted by the Professor of Divinity at Glasgow University that he horse-whipped that luckless divine in front of his class. For his pains he was charged with assault and sentenced to fourteen days in Glasgow's Barlinnie Prison. When the two weeks were up, a delegation of the men went to James Weir with the uncompromising message, 'We're no at the work tomorrow,' explaining that 'Jim was comin' oot of the jail.' Accompanied by a brass band, they met him and carried him on their shoulders across Glasgow to Cathcart. In later years he became a director of the Bank of England, thus certainly becoming the only member of that august body to have served time in one of HM prisons. J.G. was also very observant. It was he who, at lunch with the other directors one day in the 1920s, spotted something unusual about the cauliflower. It transpired that one of the cooks had gone insane and had attempted to kill the directors by putting ground glass in the vegetables.

The company was notably international in its outlook. This was not solely because, as the shipbuilding industry developed in other countries, it was commercially necessary to be so. From an early age William Weir was keen to learn from what was happening in the USA and France by way of technical advances in design and materials, and particularly in manufacturing methods, and he made frequent fact-finding trips overseas. (One story has it that on returning from France to report on competitors there, he described the main French firms, but said he had been unable to find out anything about one in particular who had a good number of offices bearing the words 'Pompes Funèbres'.) His first visit to the USA was at the age of twenty. He paid £2 for the fare, but he could sleep only when the fifth engineer was on watch, as they had just one bunk between the two of them.

In the age of the jet we take the ease of long distance travel for granted. It was less easy in those days. J. G. Weir recounted visiting Japan shortly before the First World War. He went by the quick route, which involved taking the Trans Siberian Railway to Port Arthur, or Lushun, in China, and then a ship to Yokohama. During the first part of the journey, his train came to a halt in the middle of an immense snow covered forest. The guard then appeared, carrying a number of axes, and informed the male passengers that they had run out of coal, and if they wished to proceed on their way they should set about chopping some wood so that the locomotive could get to the next station.

America made a lasting impression on William Weir. On an early visit he met Henry Ford, who showed him his new and revolutionary car factory. On another occasion he was so impressed by the light machine shop of the Packard Car Company that he bought the drawings of the building for $500 and then had a copy of it built at Cathcart. It was the first reinforced concrete building in Scotland, and as no local contractor had done such work before, Weir's hired labour and built it themselves. It became a listed building and remained the company's head office until 2005.

Labour relations in the early part of the twentieth century were on the whole good at Cathcart in the fitting and machine shops, although less so in the foundry. There was a friendly atmosphere in the shops, and an unusual feature in the early days of the firm was the annual Weir's dinner, at which the entire workforce was entertained by the directors. As the number of employees grew, the event apparently got somewhat rowdy and out of hand, and eventually it had to be discontinued. The official reason was that it was not possible to find a venue that would accommodate everyone, but in fact it was stopped at the request of the chief constable of Glasgow.

Like the Weir family itself, the descendants of significant numbers of the early employees worked for the company for several generations. In those days, many employers in Glasgow were reluctant to have Protestants and Catholics working alongside each other, due to the often tense relations between the two communities, epitomised on the sporting field by the rivalry between the Rangers and Celtic football teams. Weir's was a Protestant shop and remained largely so until this discriminatory practice was effectively ended by direction of labour during the Second World War. The recruiting mechanism was the simple one of asking an applicant where he had gone to school: if he replied 'St Joseph's', say, then he was clearly a Catholic and was unlikely to be hired. The firm's sympathies were always pretty clear, as William Weir was Honorary President of Rangers for many years.

Drinking was a serious problem in Glasgow in those days as much as it is today. At that time there was a system called 'local option', under which a parish could elect to be 'dry'. On several occasions, the Weir's management encouraged this option in Cathcart, at times with success. It is only fair to remark, however, that the problem was not confined to the shop floor. Indeed, during one forty-year period of the firm's history, either at Cathcart or its main subsidiaries, a sales director, a production director, a personnel director, a works manager and a finance director all had to leave as a consequence of excessive drinking.

During the period up to 1914, Weir's stuck mainly to its established business. It did, however, continue with related developments. One of these was the high-speed turbine-driven centrifugal boiler-feed pump, which was made necessary by the considerable increase in the size of boilers, for which the established reciprocating feed pumps had become very large and cumbersome. (One of these large feed pumps manufactured by Weir's is clearly visible in underwater photographs of the wreck of the *Titanic*.) A brilliant but somewhat eccentric German engineer called Peitermuller was engaged to work on the new pump design. His design ran at the then unheard-of speed for a pump of 10,000 rpm. The difficulty in finding a material for the impeller (the device by which energy was transmitted to the fluid being pumped) was to lead subsequently to the involvement of Weir's with the International Nickel Company in the USA and production of Monel metal.

Another interesting activity at the time was the supply of oil pipeline pumps, first to the Burmah Oil Company and subsequently to the Anglo Persian Oil Company, the progenitor of BP. The latter contract was a dramatic story in itself. For £25,000, Weir's undertook to supply the equipment for the pumping stations and to supervise the erection and the construction of the pipeline from the first oil well at Maiden-i-Naftun down to Abadan on the Gulf. Anglo Persian provided the bolted iron pipe as a free issue, and paid for the local labour of some 3,000 tribesmen. It was a big job, so Weir's originally sent out two men to manage the project; Charles Ritchie, who subsequently became general manager of Anglo Persian, and Jamieson, his assistant, who later succeeded him in the same post. J. G. Weir joined them later. How different the management of such a project would be today, when dozens of highly paid expatriates would be needed, even when working under infinitely easier conditions. There were indeed giants in those days.

There was no port at Abadan, so the pumping station boilers were dropped in the sea and towed ashore by rowing boats. They were then rolled some 150 miles across the desert. At the site there were huge pools of crude oil held back with sand dams. When the line was completed and had to be tested, the locals had a habit of going out at night and loosening the bolts so that they would then be hired again to tighten them up. Ritchie despaired of managing the consequent leaks, so, taking his best camel, he rode to where the telegraph line ran between the UK and India and wired a laconic telegram home, saying, 'Send one Blériot monoplane with instruction book.'

Weir's duly obliged, paying £1,500 for the machine. Ritchie assembled the plane, in spite of the instructions being in French, which he did not understand. He then distilled his own fuel (how many people today could manage that?) and cleared some ground as an airfield. Alas, his skill as a pilot did not match his courage in undertaking this hazardous enterprise, and he crashed. A dramatic photo of the wreckage exists, but the aircraft must have been repaired, as it hung for some years in the offices of the Kuwait Oil Company in London and is now in the Science Museum. Ritchie had to continue inspecting the pipeline for leaks from his camel rather than by air.

William Weir was an early automobile enthusiast, and this led to the firm's only departure at that time from its established business. He was a founder of the Royal Scottish Automobile Club, owned the second car in Scotland (licence number G4), drove in early motor races (including the French Grand Prix), and was a shareholder in Darracq, a leading French car maker. As a result, a negotiation took place with the Hon. C. S. Rolls, with the object of forming a car company to be called Rolls Weir. When the plan fell through, Rolls teamed up instead with Henry Royce, a Manchester engineer and crane builder. Given Royce's subsequent great distinction as an aircraft engine designer, culminating in the Rolls Royce Merlin, it is ironic that one of his overhead cranes is still in service at Weir's. Such is one of history's 'might have beens'.

Subsequently Weir's became involved in the Darracq Serpollet steam bus. Not only did they make the buses, but they also invested in a London bus company (an ingenious if undesirable way to guarantee sales) that ran them in competition with the London General Omnibus Company. Alas, this diversification ended in failure. The Serpollets were not well designed and apparently could manage only 2 mph uphill. Eventually Darracq foundered, but only after Weir's had built three Darracq-designed racing cars from scratch in six weeks for the Gordon Bennett Trophy races in the Isle of Man. As none of them moved far, if at all, from the starting line perhaps it is fortunate that Weir's stuck with their main business. Nevertheless, such was the talent of Weir's senior management at that time, and the quality of their production methods compared with those of almost all the early motor manufacturers, that a quite different story might have developed.

The period from 1890 to the outbreak of the First World War in 1914 was one of financial success. Profits were £38,000 on sales of £188,000 in 1900; £168,000 on sales of £534,000 in 1910; and £338,000 on sales of £1,294,000 in 1914. (Such sums may seem modest today, but would perhaps be some 40 or 50 times more if expressed in present-day terms.) The profit margins and return on capital were obviously excellent, and when J. D. Latta resigned as sales director in 1917, he said he had rarely sold anything for less than twice what it cost to make. Some years were naturally more difficult than others; in 1908 there was a severe recession in merchant ship building, but this was somewhat cushioned by the large naval programme of the time, not only for the Royal Navy but for those foreign powers who built warships in Britain or whose own shipyards imported Weir's equipment or made it under licence.

The naval fleets of most countries (apart from the USA

and France) were at this time principally equipped with Weir's equipment, whether made in Cathcart or by Weir licensees such as Atlas Werke in Germany or Mitsubishi and Kawasaki in Japan. Such licences were highly profitable. In Japan, for example, the licensees guaranteed that over half the requirements were imported from Cathcart, and on the remainder a royalty of 15 per cent on UK selling price was paid. Relations with the Imperial Japanese Navy were particularly cordial, especially with their Admiral Fujii, and training of Japanese engineers was carried out at Cathcart. Japan was of course an ally of Britain at that time, as it was in the First World War also. Admiral Fujii, however, came to a sad end. Early in 1914, William Weir and the heads of C. A. Parsons and Babcocks were asked to a very private meeting with the chairman of Vickers, who explained that he had a most delicate problem. Vickers had built in Barrow a battleship for the Japanese, but Admiral Fujii refused to sign for the ship, and thus trigger the substantial final payment, unless he personally received a significant commission. The other suppliers were asked to contribute, and this they reluctantly did, but the shameful transaction was somehow revealed and the admiral, in the best samurai tradition, committed harakiri on the quarterdeck of the new vessel.

The outbreak of the First World War brought great changes to Weir's. The company was of course a key supplier to the Royal Navy, from whom there was a continuing demand for its products, and as the war went on and merchant ships were sunk, that also created a need for replacement equipment. Weir's had considerable extra capacity, however, and were not therefore likely to find it difficult to meet even a strong demand for its traditional products. In the first days of the war, William Weir was able to reassure the Engineer-in-Chief of the Fleet, Admiral Sir Henry Oram, on this score.

But whereas the Royal Navy was well prepared for war, the same could not be said of the army or, as time went on, the fledgling Royal Flying Corps. The professional army was highly trained and efficient, but it was not large, and little thought or preparation had been given to meeting the huge demand for equipment and munitions which rapidly developed as the army grew greatly in numbers to meet urgent commitments on the Western Front and elsewhere. The professional armament makers such as Vickers, Armstrong Whitworth and Beardmore's were good companies, but they could not possibly expand quickly enough to meet the new demand. It was therefore for the rest of the engineering industry to plug the gap. Government and much of that industry had no proper plan at all for doing this, and approached the problem, at least in the early part of the war, with distinct complacency. Two men, however, David Lloyd George (Minister of Munitions at the start of the war) and William Weir, quickly understood that this was the first total war, and would be fought as much between fully mobilised economies as it was on the battlefield and at sea.

Very early in 1915, Weir's response was to take on a large contract for shell production, mainly 8-inch artillery shells. No one had envisaged that warfare on the Western Front would develop in the way it did. The widespread use by both sides of the machine gun and barbed wire meant that frontal assault by infantry was either largely ineffective or very costly in casualties, not that this seemed to stop the high command from continuing for years with such tactics. (The deadly role of the machine gun is affirmed by the memorial to the Machine Gun Corps at Hyde Park Corner in London. It depicts David leaning on Goliath's sword, flanked by two machine guns, and carries the chilling inscription, 'Saul hath slain his thousands, but David his tens of thousands.')

Accordingly the Western Front soon developed into a war fought from fixed entrenched positions, and assaults by both sides were either supported or repelled by immense artillery barrages. It did not occur to the generals that this was in a sense partly counter-productive, since one's own side's offensive barrage often made the ground so cratered and muddy as to be almost impassable for the attacking troops.

One result of this development was a tremendous demand for shells and intermittent severe shortages, starting as early as March 1915. Later in the war these shortages were a factor in the fall of Herbert Asquith's Government and Lloyd George's elevation to power.

Weir's consequently set about shell manufacture in earnest. Two specialist factories called Albert and Flanders were put up at Cathcart, and the company announced that, after deduction of their expenses, any profits would go to the Red Cross and similar organisations. However, they soon faced a very serious and intractable problem. Whereas many workmen volunteered enthusiastically to join the army, among some of those who remained in industry there was a radical element, particularly in part of the trades union leadership, and notably on the Clyde, who took a very different view, epitomised by those Labour Party heroes, the Clyde Workers Committee. Not only did the more dedicated socialists consider that the war was a capitalist affair and none of their business, but many staunch trades unionists felt that the protection of their skilled-worker status against the unskilled, and women in particular, was as important as the war. Indeed, many in the unions looked at the labour shortage as an opportunity to press for higher pay. This was particularly the case in the shipyards, hence the saying in Govan, 'She's marrying into the nobility. She's marrying a riveter.'

William Weir reacted to this in the strongest terms. He considered the unions to be downright unpatriotic and their attitude to be evil and insulting to their fellows who were fighting on the front. The first confrontation came very early in the war, in February 1915, when 8,000 men, including 2,000 from Weir's, went on strike for a pay claim. The troubles continued after the Munitions of War Act was passed soon afterwards, but the unions' action against dilution, culminating in the strike at Beardmore's armament works in the spring of 1916, was broken by severe measures, including the threat of conscripting strikers to the front.

William Weir had come to the attention of Lloyd George in 1915, after some rather pompous industrialist had written to the papers in a complacent tone saying that industry in Scotland was 'ready and prepared to do its bit'. Weir had replied in highly caustic terms, saying that industry did not in fact have the slightest idea of what was required of it. Lloyd George saw Weir's letter, and as a result prevailed upon him to leave the firm early in 1915 to become a temporary civil servant.

In William Weir's absence, the management of Weir's was taken over by John Richmond and C. R. Lang, and in 1916 the firm took on the quite new and radical task of aircraft manufacture. Unlike most companies engaged in this, they did not simply make engines or parts to be assembled elsewhere by professional aircraft constructors, but instead built the entire aircraft, including the engines. The planes were built to the aircraft designers' drawings on production line principles, and much of the work was carried out by women.

In his new government role, William Weir was first of all put in charge of munitions production in Scotland, and then, when the Royal Flying Corps started a rapid expansion and there were great difficulties in producing enough aircraft, he took responsibility for this as well. Later in the war, when the Royal Air Force was set up in place of the Royal Flying Corps as an independent service, William Weir became Secretary of State for Air and a member of the War Cabinet, and was created Lord Weir. The job of managing aircraft production was taken over by his brother, J. G. Weir, who had been an early pioneer flyer, gaining his licence in 1912. J.G. had joined the RFC and become a brigadier at the age of 30, converting to air commodore when the RAF was formed.

At the beginning of 1918, William Weir took over the Air Ministry from the 1st Lord Cowdray. Cowdray was Weetman Pearson; originally from Yorkshire, he became the most famous contractor of his time. He completed the flooded Holland Tunnel in New York when everyone said it couldn't be done, and subsequently drained the marshes of Mexico City, built the port of Vera Cruz, and founded the Mexican oil industry through Mexican Eagle. While William Weir discussed the handover of the air force, Lady Weir had tea with Lady Cowdray who, at a moment when the war was going very badly for the allies, astounded her guest with the remark, 'I hardly know how we can carry on. There are only fifty-one staff left.'

By the end of the war, Weir's had turned out no fewer than 1,140 planes, many of them de Havilland DH9s, together with many aircraft components, such as aluminium engine blocks, for other firms. People often tend to think of the First World War almost entirely in terms of trench warfare and do not realise the extent of air warfare; by the end of 1918, the Royal Air Force in fact had 290,000 personnel, 700 airfields and over 23,000 aircraft. Sadly, these high figures were matched by a fearful rate of casualties among the pilots; in April 1917 the average life expectancy of a fighter pilot was a mere 92 flying hours.

By the end of the war, the Cathcart factory had greatly expanded. Employment, which had peaked at around 3,000 before the war, had risen to over 6,000, of whom 2,000 were women.

2

Between the wars
1919–39

Peace brought its own problems. For two or three years after the First World War it is true that there was a considerable boom in merchant shipbuilding, to replace the heavy losses inflicted by German submarines, but naval construction naturally almost ceased. This was a very heavy blow, and the decline was later formalised by the Washington Treaty, which attempted to set permanent limits on the size of navies. Naval shipbuilding did not recover until rearmament began in the mid 1930s. From 1922 there was a severe recession in merchant shipbuilding, which continued until the 1930s, with only a slight recovery in 1928. A dramatic and visible result of this recession could be seen when work stopped on the half-completed *Queen Mary* at John Brown in Clydebank. In the face of this calamitous decline in its major market, Weir's clearly had to find new activities.

The first of these was a highly imaginative venture into housing. As hardly any new houses had been built during the war, there was by 1919 an acute housing shortage. Lord Weir believed that the solution did not lie with the building industry, but instead in applying engineering principles of mass production to prefabricating houses in factories and using unconventional materials such as sheet steel cladding and timber framing. Prototypes were designed and built. A public demonstration was organised in a small square near Victoria Station, loaned for the purpose by the Duke of Westminster. Stands were erected for the public to watch, and one of the new houses was put up in 24 hours. Finally a couple moved in, complete with a plastic baby, to applause from the crowd.

Success would seem to have been assured, but this did not take account of William Weir's old foes, the trades unions, in this case the building unions. Ostensibly they objected to the fact that the houses were built by engineers, whose rates of pay were lower than in the building trades, but arguably they, and indeed most building employers with them, simply objected to this new competition. Accordingly, the unions not only exerted strong and effective pressure on local authorities not to buy the houses, but they blacked work on foundations. The whole enterprise therefore became extremely difficult for Weir's. They did manage to build some 3,000 houses, but then reluctantly had to abandon the effort and close the housing factory at Cardonald. Financially, the net result of the whole enterprise was a profit of £5. Although these steel houses were originally intended to have a life of only 25 years, since there were initial doubts about the potential life of the steel shells, quite a few were still occupied some sixty years after they were built.

Weir's next effort to develop a new line of business was in metallurgy. In 1910, Lord Weir had gone to the USA to try to find a material that would meet the arduous operating conditions of the new turbo feed pump, and he visited the International Nickel Company (or Inco). He was shown a propeller for a destroyer in a nickel alloy called

Monel, named after Ambrose Monel, one of the company's founders and also a famous flyfisher for salmon. A licence was taken from Inco for alloys like Monel, covering the British Empire and part of Europe. A factory was built in Thornliebank, and Weir's set about developing a business in Monel components. Sophisticated alloy steels had not been much developed at the time, and there was therefore a market for such products as corrosion-resistant condenser tubes, turbine blading and other applications. The business developed so well that in the 1930s Weir's had to decide whether to concentrate on engineering or on metals. Probably wisely – as new stainless steels were then emerging – they sold the business to Inco. For many years after that, William Weir and subsequently his son Kenneth served as directors of Inco.

One consequence of the sale to Inco was that Weir's were allowed to sell nickel itself in France. This was probably a way for Inco to access the French market without directly confronting their rivals Le Nickel, with whom they may have had some arrangement in those days regarding the territories in which they operated. Weir's manager in France was a Monsieur Foianesi, a Swiss. In 1945, at the end of the Second World War, Foianesi came over to visit Cathcart, and to Kenneth Weir's amazement asked what he should do with his stock of nickel. Apparently Foianesi had a close friend in the French railway system, who, knowing that nickel was a strategic material in desperately short supply for the Germans, had the stocks loaded on to rail trucks and shuffled around various remote rural railway sidings for the duration of the war. Post-war, it was a very tidy windfall.

Monel metal and housing, the first venture successful, but the second abortive, were not the only steps Weir's took in the 1920s and early 1930s to counter the drastic recession in shipbuilding. This recession was made even worse for British shipyards by increased protectionism and by subsidies from foreign governments for their own shipbuilding industries. In 1920, Weir's entered the compressor business by purchasing the Glasgow firm of Murray, Workman, and this gave them a product needed by the increasing number of ships driven by diesel engines. In 1921, Weir's obtained a diesel engine licence from Sulzer Bros in Switzerland, but this proved difficult to exploit, as quite a number of shipyards were themselves already licensed diesel engine builders. Nor did Weir's help their own cause when they took the very eccentric decision to redesign some key features of the Sulzer machines.

More important than these initiatives was the decision to enter the rotary pump business. As it stood, Weir's pumping business was then limited by its product range to direct-acting reciprocating steam-driven pumps, and its rotary pump activities were confined to turbine-driven centrifugal boiler-feed pumps and later to motor-driven multistage boiler-feed pumps for power stations. Given the serious problems of shipbuilding and the increased proportion of diesel ships (which required far less auxiliary machinery compared with steam ships), Weir's obviously faced a serious decline in their traditional markets. They could have tried to develop their own range of rotary pumps, but that would have taken considerable time and expense. Their decision at the end of the First World War to purchase for £45,000 a 50 per cent share in Drysdale's, located in Glasgow at Yoker, on the other side of the Clyde from Cathcart, was therefore unquestionably the right one.

Drysdale's had an excellent reputation, a wide range of products, good profits and a competent management, particularly in the persons of John Drysdale and subsequently

John Young. Their management was not, however, without its eccentricities. John Drysdale and his brother quite frequently disagreed and settled their differences by putting on boxing gloves and going a round or two on the office roof. What modern writers on the theory of management would have thought of this unusual method of resolving boardroom differences is hard to imagine. Age, incidentally, did nothing much to calm John Drysdale's temperament, and in later years he got into trouble when he shot at a trespasser who was cutting down a Christmas tree in his garden.

Investment in Drysdale's brought to Weir's a product line which eventually included many applications, including large pumps for condenser cooling water, drydock pumps, and pumps for water supply, firefighting, sewage, sanitary and water works service, transformer cooling, salvage, oil cargo and many other uses. Drysdale's gave their pumps somewhat odd names: the 'Vampire' dealt with hospital waste and other insalubrious material, while the 'Snorer' was a salvage pump.

Other important initiatives immediately after the war related to Weir's foundries. The iron foundry in Cathcart was not only crucial to Weir's production flow, but was also an important cost factor. Labour relations in the foundry were very poor, and the National Union of Foundry Workers and the Associated Ironmoulders were stupid and intransigent, particularly in their attitude towards adopting new methods or using unskilled labour for even the most mundane of tasks. William Weir proposed that the whole foundry operation be reorganised, and that payment by results should be introduced, pointing out that the business as it stood was quite uncompetitive. Indeed, he made the point that the cost of castings at Cathcart was twice that of castings in Philadelphia, where the workforce were paid

twice as much. The men and their union would not nego-
tiate, however, and accordingly the brief post-war shipping
boom did not benefit Weir's nearly as much as it ought to
have done, because in the face of strikes and poor foundry
output they had to buy in castings, with often deplorable
results.

Weir's answer was to purchase land nearby at Thornliebank, incorporate a new company called Argus Foundry
Limited, order modern plant from the USA and start up an
operation which required no skilled operators at all. Certainly this solved the problem as far as smaller-sized castings
were concerned, and in time the business even had a certain
amount of success in obtaining work from third parties.

No history of Weir's in the interwar period would be
complete without mention of their involvement in rotat-
ing-wing aircraft. Today, we take the helicopter for granted,
but few people know of Weir's involvement in it. Financially, this was far from a success for the company. Rather
like Weir's brief enthusiasm for automobiles before the war,
it was driven as much by the attraction of a completely new
technology as by any careful analysis of the business prospects of the venture. The pioneer who excited Weir's interest was a Spaniard, Juan de la Cierva. J. G. Weir saw an early
demonstration flight by one of de la Cierva's autogiros in
1925 at Farnborough. The Cierva Autogiro Company was
subsequently formed, with J. G. Weir, Sir Robert Kindersley and others putting up the capital.

Although Lord Weir supported his brother's enthusiasm,
Weir's as a company did not involve themselves financially
in the autogiro until 1933. Originally, the autogiro had stub
wings and a conventionally mounted propeller, and the
rotor was unpowered. The Cierva Company was initially
only a design and licensing business, but after the death of
Cierva in 1936 it became a manufacturer and even

developed its own aircraft engines. At the same time, the basic autogiro principle was abandoned and development of true helicopters began. J. G. Weir was always the leading force in the venture. He frequently commuted to work at Cathcart in an autogiro, and his wife Mora, whom he had met in 1918 when he had crashed in a field on her father's estate in Fife, was the first woman to have a licence to fly a rotating wing machine — a foolhardy venture, as she was a notably unskilled driver even of a motor car. In the original 1935 film of *The Thirty-Nine Steps*, the villains can be seen hunting for Richard Hannay on the moors of Galloway in a Weir's autogiro — and J. G. Weir flew the machine.

As far as their traditional activities were concerned, Weir's made a number of acquisitions. In 1928 they bought Contraflo Engineering, a long-time competitor in condensing and feed heating plant. This was not simply to eliminate a competitor, but as much to obtain the services of Harold Hillier, Contraflo's chief engineer, who became Weir's technical director in 1933. Also in 1933 they bought for £50,000 the assets of Messrs Mumford, whose boiler feed regulator was an important addition to their product range.

From 1921 to 1934, shipbuilding was in serious recession. Unemployment in the industry was over 60 per cent, and the nadir was reached in 1932 when a mere 72,000 tons of shipping was laid down. As there was very little naval construction, the only compensation for Weir's during this period was the programme of power station construction, in which the company played an increasing part, supplying feed pumps, condensing and feed heating equipment and Drysdale pumps.

During the early 1930s, Weir's endeavoured to attack the US market. On their own account they managed to obtain the order for the boiler feed pumps for the Hell's Gate power station of Consolidated Edison, which had what was then the largest generator in the world at 100MW. Through a licensee, the Aldrich Pump Co. of Pennsylvania, they even won some feed pump orders from the US Navy, most notably for the famous aircraft carriers USS *Wasp* and USS *Hornet*.

Financially, the whole of this period was a difficult one. Losses were made in some years between 1920 and 1925, and profit in 1930 (the best year until recovery eventually started in 1935) was a mere £142,000. The company was never, however, in the slightest danger of collapse, as was the case with so many others. It had started the period with a very strong balance sheet. So strong was it, in fact, that not only could it make the investments and acquisitions mentioned, such as Monel Weir and Argus Foundry, but in 1923 it repaid its entire preference capital of £600,000, and in 1929 repaid £4 per ordinary share while prevailing on Drysdale's to take similar action. It could not be said, though, that Weir's found any way of avoiding all the consequences of the Depression. Hatches were battened down, the business was shrunk, and working capital was reduced in the hope that one day the storm would subside.

And in 1934 the horizon did indeed begin to lighten. Work restarted on the *Queen Mary*, as a result of William Weir's report to the Prime Minister, Stanley Baldwin, on the transatlantic passenger trade, and the subsequent merger that he organised between the Cunard and White Star lines. (William Weir later remarked that one of the main difficulties he faced in this negotiation was getting hold of the Cunard directors, as they apparently spent much of their time hunting in Cheshire.) From 1935, rearmament for the Royal Navy started. Sales began to pick up, rising from the pathetic figure of £400,000 in 1933 to £2,100,000 in 1939, at which time almost 80 per cent of work was for the

Admiralty. Profits rose in line with increased sales to reach over £400,000 in 1939.

Foreign naval work also played an important part, and a large and very profitable order for the machinery of three cruisers and twelve destroyers (built to Italian Ansaldo design) was obtained from the Soviet Navy.

This was followed by an order from the Soviet oil ministry for a number of very large gas compressors. These machines were for injecting carbon dioxide into oil wells to stimulate flow, a pioneering technical development by the Russians. Progress on building them was frustratingly slow due to the extraordinarily careful procedures of the Russian inspectors. They earned the sympathy of Weir's people, however, when they eventually explained that their practice was due to the fact that they would be charged with sabotage, and probably shot, if the machines did not work.

Kenneth Weir, who negotiated the order in Russia, managed to obtain a 50 per cent down payment (which was pretty much the whole cost of manufacture) by explaining to his communist customers that, as of course they must know, capitalism was in collapse, so a firm like Weir's could not proceed without the money up front. During the whole of his time in Russia, Kenneth Weir was closely followed everywhere by a KGB agent. When he went to bed, the agent slept on the floor in front of his hotel room door. Kenneth Weir's wife was very nervous about his trip, as this was at the time when the Russians had put engineers from Vickers on trial. Indeed, while he was there, the Russians kidnapped the chief naval architect of Ansaldo and forced him to work for their own navy.

Thus, when the Second World War started, the company, having weathered the Depression, was very busy and in a prosperous state.

For the whole interwar period, however, William Weir, although remaining chairman and exercising a strong influence on major decisions, was heavily involved in public affairs and had little involvement in the day-to-day management of the business. The top management was in the hands of his brother, J. G. Weir, his half-brother Sir John Richmond, and C. R. Lang, who were joined in the 1930s by Kenneth Weir (William Weir's son) and Russell Lang (the son of C. R. Lang). From 1933, Harold Hillier became technical director, taking over this responsibility from J. G. Weir, who was by then heavily involved in Cierva Autogiro.

Lord Weir's work outside the company covered a quite remarkable range of activities. The Weir Report of 1926 reorganised the electricity supply industry and created the National Grid; another report proposed electrification of the railways; he was a father of the sugar beet industry, established to avoid the crisis that arose in the First World War when at one point only six days' supply remained in the country; he was responsible for restarting work on the *Queen Mary*, and laying down the *Queen Elizabeth*; the 'shadow factories' which played a crucial part in war production after 1939 were his brainchild in 1934 (these were factories built for a specific wartime purpose, for example aircraft engine production, and equipped with machine tools ready for use, but unmanned until the emergency came); and he played an important role in the formation of ICI, which included negotiating with Dupont on behalf of the British chemical companies. There was much more, but undoubtedly his most important role was in organising aircraft rearmament and the rapid growth of the Royal Air Force from 1935 onwards. Apart from all this he also served as a director of ICI, Shell, Lloyds Bank and the International Nickel Company.

It is interesting to speculate as to what the history of Weir's might have been had a man of his outstanding ability, intelligence and energy devoted himself single-mindedly to the fortunes of the firm. There were, in fact, at least two occasions when the company's history could have taken a quite different turn.

The first of these is described by Anthony Sampson in his book *The Anatomy of a Merger*, which covers the story of how AEI, Metropolitan Vickers, English Electric and General Electric Co were put together by Arnold Weinstock to form GEC. Few are today aware that a similar proposal was made around 1928 to amalgamate these same companies into a British electrical giant. A key role was played by the great US firms of Westinghouse and General Electric, who were substantial shareholders in parts of the UK industry. Their support for the idea was almost certainly based on the same motivation which had led Dupont to support the formation of ICI in the British chemical industry a few years earlier. The plan was to create strong and friendly British bulwarks against German industry, in this case Siemens and AEG and the former I. G. Farben, and bulwarks which were also on good terms with the Americans. Owen D. Young of General Electric made it a condition that William Weir would become chairman of the combination.

This proposal was only practical for Weir's if they also became part of the group, and as their lines of business fitted together quite well, this was not a problem for the family. The key was William Weir's own view. His brother, J. G. Weir, made it clear that if William was to become chairman, he would have to give up entirely his outside activities and devote himself full time to the new business. This, after much deliberation, William decided he was unwilling to do, mainly because he felt he still had a substantial contribution to make to national affairs. How interesting it is to speculate what the outcome might have been, and what an important opportunity was missed for British industry generally. Certainly, Weir's history would have been quite different, just as it would have been if they had, some twenty years earlier, yielded to the temptation to enter the car industry.

A second opportunity arose in 1938. Business in the USA had been even worse hit by the Depression than in Britain, and the USA had suffered a secondary slump in 1938. At that time Benjamin Guggenheim, the mining tycoon, controlled the Worthington company, Weir's principal international competitor. Guggenheim offered William Weir control of the business for $1,000,000, equivalent to about £200,000 at the time. Lord Weir could easily have found that from his personal resources, quite apart the company's. Once again he declined because of his involvement in rearmament. Again, what an interesting turn this would have given to Weir's fortunes and history, and how very ironic it was that thirty years later Weir's were to become closely involved with Worthington, and that their independence was only preserved because of the confidence that the chairman of Worthington then had in Weir.

3

The Second World War and beyond

1939–54

When war broke out again in 1939, Weir's played a very similar role to that in the previous war. Once again, they had to meet a continuous and heavy demand for machinery both for the Royal Navy and for merchant shipbuilding to replace the heavy losses inflicted by the German U-boat campaign. In the First World War, they had used their capacity to produce unfamiliar products, at that time shells and aircraft. This time they turned their hand to producing field artillery. The war also produced a heavy requirement for specialised products. For example, Drysdale's produced a great number of petrol-driven salvage pumps, needed because of the many ships which were damaged rather than sunk. Many mobile sea water evaporator units were made to supply water to the advancing armies in Africa. Zwicky, a small firm in Slough which was acquired in the 1930s and made refuelling tankers for aircraft, expanded greatly, producing over 5,000 such tankers during the war. Another product was high-powered steam turbine driven hydraulic pumps for moving the gun turrets on capital ships and for operating aircraft carrier catapults. (By a strange irony these last had originally been developed for the Imperial Japanese Navy.)

The involvement of Cathcart in artillery production was interesting. The army did not have an adequate field gun between the wars, but by December 1938 they had approved the design of the 25-pounder gun, with a maximum range of some eight miles. As a 'shadow factory', Weir's had received first an educational order and then in May 1939 a bulk order for gun carriages. The first they made was shown to the King and Queen in February 1940.

Kenneth Weir led the national effort as chairman of the 25-pounder and 6-pounder production committees from 1940. Other companies who worked with Weir's included Mackie's in Belfast, a leading textile machinery maker; Baker Perkins, the food machinery maker; W. T. Avery, who made weighing machines; the LMS locomotive works in Crewe; and Kirkstall Forge in Leeds. Kirkstall still had in occasional use the 'old hammer', a steam hammer that had been built by James Watt. It is remarkable how firms of such disparate experience adapted themselves so success-fully to making totally unfamiliar products. Over 10,000 25-pounders were built before production ceased in 1943, more than a third of them by Weir's. In parallel with 25-pounder production, Weir's were also heavily involved in the production of 6-pounder anti-tank guns, of which they produced some 2,000, and in the 17-pounder gun needed to counter the heavily armoured German Tiger tank.

One story about the 25-pounder gun is not widely known but deserves to be told. When the shadow factory arrangements were set up in 1938 it became clear that there was a shortage of the special lathes needed for rifling the gun barrels. The best lathes came from Germany. A Jewish dealer in secondhand machine tools, who had fled Hitler in 1935, bravely volunteered to return incognito to Germany, and by remarkable subterfuges managed to purchase the necessary machines and have them delivered to the UK via Switzerland. After the war Kenneth Weir tried, to no avail, to obtain an award for this gallant man. Perhaps the authorities thought it inappropriate as he had been a German alien.

During the Second World War there was fortunately no recurrence of the labour problems which had blighted the early part of the previous war. No doubt much of this was due to the appointment of Ernest Bevin, a profoundly patriotic Labour politician, as Minister of Labour. Weir's problems were limited to absenteeism, particularly after holidays. At the height of the war, Weir's employed 5,200 men and women at all their establishments, compared with 6,000 at Cathcart alone in the First World War.

As in the First World War, the most senior members of management were wholly or partly seconded from the firm. For the first three years, Lord Weir was involved in war production, first as chairman of the Tank Board and then as Director General of Explosives. J. G. Weir was in Washington for three years with the Allied Purchasing Commission, in charge of aircraft procurement, and temporarily headed the commission when its chairman, Arthur Purvis, was killed. Kenneth Weir, as previously noted, was for most of the war involved in artillery production, and Harold Hillier, the technical director, was, apart from his duties at Weir's, also technical consultant to the Director of Artillery.

Statistically, sales during the war — except for war production such as artillery, which was on an 'agency and no profit' basis – were around £2.5–3 million each year for Cathcart alone. Profits before tax were very high in 1939, at over £600,000, but averaged about £450,000 a year to the end of the war. On a net profits basis they were, due to excess profits tax, understandably much lower, and indeed for the three years of 1941–3, net profit was hardly 25 per cent of profit before tax.

Clearly Weir's contribution to key parts of war production was very important, and the company has always been justifiably very proud of its war work. It could, however, be said, in a quiet and modest way, in keeping with the man involved, that perhaps the firm's most important contribution of all to the outcome of the Second World War was in fact that which their own chairman had made in the years before the conflict. As we have seen, as early as 1934, when hardly anyone was thinking about another war, William Weir had been instrumental in setting up the whole concept of 'shadow factories' for war production. And when the 1938 Empire Exhibition took place in Glasgow, in which he was much involved, he insisted that the large 'Palace of Engineering' should be of bolted construction so that it could be reassembled as an aircraft factory. (It is still at Prestwick Airport to this day.) From 1935 to 1938 he was responsible for aircraft rearmament and the expansion of the RAF: in 1936 he persuaded the Government to reorganise armament production for the army by appointing Vice Admiral Sir Harold Brown, the retired Engineer-in-Chief of the Royal Navy, as Director General of Munitions Production at the War Office, a department that subsequently was the basis of the wartime Ministry of Supply. It must have taken considerable efforts to persuade the army to have a retired naval officer in charge of producing their weapons. Apart from all that, in later life he confided to me that one of the arguments he had advanced privately to

Stanley Baldwin for restarting work on the *Queen Mary* and for laying down the *Queen Elizabeth* was the strategic one that in time of war each ship could carry an entire US division across the Atlantic in four days – which was exactly what the two ships finally did.

The aftermath of the Second World War brought great changes to Weir's. In 1945 they bought out the 50 per cent of Drysdale's which they did not already own. They then became a public company in 1946, the flotation being handled by National and Schroders as merchant bankers, and Rowe and Pitman as stockbrokers. The main reason for this was that the senior directors, who were also the main shareholders, were getting on in years, and the uncomfortable and looming prospect of heavy death duties (for which few steps towards mitigation had been taken) was a serious potential problem for a private company. Once Weir's went public, J. W. Drysdale became a deputy chairman, alongside Sir John Richmond and J. G. Weir. N. M. Niven (a cousin of the film star David Niven) from Drysdale's also joined the board, and Kenneth Weir became managing director.

Weir's were only one of many companies who became publicly quoted at this time. The problem was not simply that of inheritance taxes at extortionate rates of 90 per cent or more. Income tax on companies and individuals was also very high. Even before the Second World War, Weir's had twice had serious difficulty with the tax authorities in maintaining their favoured and conservative policy of retaining as much of their profits as possible, and had been forced to make higher dividend distributions than they wanted. These results of the socialist government's ideological emphasis on the redistribution of wealth, rather than its creation, had two important longer term consequences which are still with us. In the first place, Britain never preserved or developed the same wide range of privately owned middle sized manufacturers, often in engineering, which Germany successfully did and which are still the backbone of the German economy. The second consequence was a social one. Locally based companies provide leaders of local communities – and indeed often benefactors – and where there are fewer such companies, the adverse result is obvious. In the mid nineteenth century, it was said with some justification that 'what Manchester thinks today, London thinks tomorrow'. That has not held true for a long time now. The resulting concentration of economic power and influence in London is hardly healthy or welcome for Britain as a whole and indeed, other perhaps than in France, this concentration is very much a British phenomenon.

Unlike the period after the First World War, when there had been only a brief boom in merchant shipbuilding, from 1945 onwards there was a continuous rise in merchant shipbuilding worldwide. This was stimulated in the earlier years by replacement of tonnage sunk in the war, and later by a great expansion in oil consumption and hence in tanker construction. Immediately after the war, British shipyards still held a strong position, as there was little competition, and in 1948 they still were building over 50 per cent of the world's output.

Ironically, in the longer run this prolonged seller's market must surely have been a crucial and adverse factor leading to the decline and eventually the virtual extinction of British merchant shipbuilding. The trouble was that it was so easy to obtain orders at high prices that there was little or no incentive for the managements or men in British yards to confront the deep-seated problems of demarcation and antiquated working practices in the industry. Indeed these problems were themselves factors inhibiting investment in modern facilities and new shipbuilding methods.

Meanwhile, as the 1950s progressed, shipbuilding expanded rapidly in Japan, Germany and Sweden, with Germany overtaking the UK around 1954. Clearly this posed one problem for Weir's, as not only was it inherently more difficult to obtain orders overseas, but also competitors who manufactured similar machinery in these countries grew in parallel with their native shipbuilding industries. Another problem was the increased size and reliability of diesel engines, which led to an increasing share of the total market being taken by motor ships instead of steam, the former requiring far less of the auxiliary machinery in Weir's product range. As in the 1920s, naval shipbuilding had again dropped off dramatically, and between 1947 and 1949 it was less than 10 per cent of Weir's output, before reviving in the 1950s with the Korean conflict and the Cold War.

This revival in traditional naval work was very important. Margins were good, although the attention which had to be paid to the high standards and detailed design requirements, and the consequent diversion of technical and managerial effort, offset this to some degree. For at least twenty more years, however, naval work was a very important activity, declining only when the size of the Royal Navy began to diminish and when gas turbines began to replace steam for ship propulsion, in the same way that diesel engines had earlier taken over from steam in merchant ships.

The Royal Navy was not the only important customer, even if it was always much the largest. The Royal Netherlands Navy was a significant customer for Weir's equipment. Before the war they had often used indigenous machinery, mainly supplied by the eminent firm of Stork-Werkspoor. During the war, however, this had proved a serious problem, as Holland was under German occupation, and home-sourced spare parts and replacements were impossible to obtain. Accordingly they decided in future to standardise on Weir's machinery. Weir's agent in Holland was Gerard de Bruyn, a most capable gentleman. He enjoyed a very high rate of commission on sales, at 10 per cent. So successful was he that he was supposedly the only person in Holland, apart from their Queen, to have a Rolls Royce. Alas, when he visited Cathcart his chauffeur almost destroyed this splendid vehicle by colliding in fog with a tramcar in the town of Barrhead. When he came over to Scotland it became the custom always to ask him by what route he had come, in order to elicit the invariable response, 'Flushing by steam.' Other important naval customers were the Royal Canadian Navy who built, to British designs, the St Laurent class of destroyers, and the Chilean Navy, whose major ships were traditionally named after the famous liberators of their country, Almirante Cochrane and Almirante O'Higgins.

In spite of problems, however, the period from 1945 to 1954 was one of great prosperity for Weir's. Even if British shipbuilding was losing its pre-eminence, and diesel power was growing, there was plenty of work available in the marine market, and the land business at home and abroad was buoyant on the back of large programmes of power station construction. Belgium was a particularly good market for condensing and feed heating plant and for boiler feed pumps. The head of one of the Belgian power companies had a somewhat unusual name, and Kenneth Weir was understandably taken aback on one occasion when, just before this customer came to visit Cathcart, a telegram reached him, reading simply, 'Dieu arrivera demain.' When Monsieur Dieu duly arrived, he was entertained to dinner at the Malmaison, in those days the only good restaurant in Glasgow. That evening, however, coincided with the annual visit to Glasgow of a unique highland figure, Gilstrap

McRae, proprietor of the wonderful and famous castle of Eilean Donan, set in the sea. This laird's once-yearly pilgrimage to Glasgow required him to be accompanied wherever he went by a waiter carrying a tray with a glass and a bottle of whisky. McRae was at the next table to M. Dieu and Kenneth Weir and myself. Soon, all conversation ceased in the restaurant as the customers watched McRae attempting to eat a plate of oysters. In the laird's happy state, many of the bivalves fell from his fork, but whenever he captured one he loudly exclaimed, 'Got him!' What M. Dieu felt about Scots we shall never know, but happily his orders continued despite his interesting experience.

On land, sea water distillation plants also began to provide an increasing and profitable market. Another positive factor for Weir's was the growth in the tanker market. For a longer period than for general cargo ships, these continued to be steam driven, and apart from the machinery required for propulsion they also needed cargo handling systems, and here Drysdale pumps driven by Weir auxiliary turbines had a ready market. The scale of demand can be seen from Shell's order, either for its own account or for charterers, of 72 identical tankers to a design by Cammell Laird, the Birkenhead shipbuilders, all specified with Weir's and Drysdale's gear. Another bonus for Weir's was the construction of many large passenger steam ships for Cunard, Canadian Pacific, Holland America and other lines.

The worst problem facing Weir's, at both Cathcart and at Drysdale's Yoker factory, was therefore that of meeting deliveries. Kenneth Weir, as managing director, recounted that he spent far more time urging on suppliers than in winning customers. To meet this, heavy investment was made in both main factories. In 1951, a new factory, Weir Valves, was also set up at the Queenslie Industrial Estate, east of Glasgow, to which a considerable amount of lighter work was contracted, although its potential contribution was later significantly negated by taking on a very large contract to build sophisticated special valves for the gaseous diffusion plant at Capenhurst, where weapons-grade uranium was produced. Meeting deliveries and quoting competitive delivery dates nevertheless continued to be a serious difficulty, and this naturally gave an opening to new competitors.

The difficulties of limited capacity and of meeting demand were exacerbated from 1952 onwards as large land-based sea water distillation contracts were won, first in Kuwait and Aden and then in the Netherlands Antilles. The Aden plant was for the Anglo-Iranian (now BP) refinery, built there at great speed to replace Abadan after Prime Minister Mohammed Mossadeq nationalised the Iranian oil industry in 1951. The main contractor for this was the American firm of Bechtel. On one occasion, one of their expeditors was harassing a fitter at Cathcart to hurry up putting together a final shipment of parts. He was met with the retort, 'Awa' wi you, we were building these things when you folk were still cowboys.'

A notable customer was the Ruler of Kuwait. When the first sea water distillation plant was built there, he came to open it. Sections of red carpet were rolled out in front of him on the desert. As he passed over them, the rear ones were rolled up by minions, who then rushed out in front of him and unrolled them again. Once he reached the plant he was ceremoniously handed a glass of newly produced fresh water. After tasting some of it he handed the glass containing the remainder to an aide. Apparently it was then taken back to the palace to be tasted again after a day or two to ensure it had not turned back into sea water. The Ruler came to Britain for the Queen's Coronation and stayed with William Weir, who gave a dinner party for him.

Those present recall the Ruler's memorable remark when his host said what good fortune it was to have discovered oil. The Ruler simply said, 'I was born in a tent in the desert and we had no money. One day a successor of mine will be born in a tent and he will have no money.' This sentiment was the rationale behind the Kuwait Investment Office, through which a substantial portion of the oil revenues was put away for the future.

Another eminent customer around that time for desalination plant was J. Paul Getty. In his dealings with Weir's, he demonstrated both his reluctance to delegate and his parsimony. When he acquired the oil concession in the Neutral Zone, a strip of land between Kuwait and Saudi Arabia, he needed water. So he phoned up Weir's himself. The operator wanted to put him through to the sales department, but he was having none of this. He said he did not deal with salesmen, and wanted to speak to 'your top evaporator man'. Duly he was put through to Eddie Paterson, the head designer of that department. For a number of weeks long conversations took place, and numerous proposals for the most up-to-date plants were put to the billionaire. Always they were too expensive. Eventually he bought from a shipbreaker a second-hand plant which had come from a scrapped battleship, and Weir's got a small order to put it into working condition.

In parallel with everything which was happening at Cathcart and at the Yoker works, the Weir Housing Corporation had been formed in 1944, marking Weir's re-entry into the field which they had unsuccessfully pioneered in the 1920s. This time, however, they had no recurrence of the union problems they had then faced, mainly because they were invited to help meet the housing shortage by two staunch Labour politicians in the shape of Tom Johnston and Arthur Woodburn. In 1944, Weir's received an

order for 5,000 council houses designed with steel framing
and cladding. They rapidly built up production, but after a
period the shortage of steel was such that they had to
abandon its use. Instead they moved to either all-timber
houses, prefabricated in their plant at Coatbridge, or timber
frame houses with prefabricated internals and conventional
exteriors. For the best part of twenty years, Weir Housing
was a highly profitable business that made a substantial
contribution to the company's earnings.

After the war Cierva also resumed operations. During
the war, little work had been done in the UK on helicopters, as it had been agreed that the Americans should handle
this part of the war effort. Indeed, early in the war a senior
official in the Air Ministry had said that 'the helicopter was
of no conceivable military significance'. As a result, US
companies such as Sikorsky gained a commanding lead
which they have never relinquished. Nevertheless, a small
machine called the Skeeter had been developed by Weir's,
and later went into production, as did another, far more
ambitious project for the Air Ministry, the Airhorse. This
was a very large machine with three rotors, designed for an
all-up weight of almost eight tons. It flew at the Farnborough Show in 1949 and that year met its specification.
Unfortunately, it crashed in 1950 in a demonstration flight,
killing the test pilots. Effectively that marked the end of
Weir's involvement in helicopters, although J. G. Weir continued on a private basis. Cierva was sold to Sanders Roe,
and subsequently its efforts and Sanders Roe's became the
basis for Westland's position today as a British helicopter
company.

In financial terms, the period from the end of the
Second World War up to 1954 was very rewarding. Profits
before tax rose without a break from just under £500,000
in 1947 to a peak of over £3 million in 1954 on sales, which

increased in that period from £6 million to £18 million. The return pre-tax on capital employed was excellent, at some 50 per cent in 1954. Tax, however, was over 50 per cent for most years.

After the war, and on becoming a public company, changes began to be made in the management of the firm. In 1946, Lord Weir was chairman, with Sir John Richmond, J. G. Weir and J. W. Drysdale as deputy chairmen. These four fulfilled in effect a largely non-executive, supervisory and advisory role. Kenneth Weir was managing director, Russell Lang works director, Harold Hillier technical director, Andrew Jamieson production director, and John Spittal and Archibald Laidlaw were finance director and sales director respectively. Neil Niven was chairman of Drysdale's and Zwicky, and Russell Lang also acted as chairman of Weir Housing and Weir Valves.

By 1953 it had become clear that the position of G. & J. Weir, both as a large business in its own right and simultaneously as a holding company, was anomalous. This was partly rationalised by appointing 'executive directors' for G. & J. Weir who were responsible only for Cathcart operations and who were not directors of the quoted company, and similar structures were put in place at Weir Housing, although they already existed at Drysdale's.

In 1954, Sir John Richmond retired at the age of 85. William Weir retired in 1955 (handing over as chairman to his son Kenneth Weir) and J. G. Weir retired in 1956. Between them, these three members of the founding family had been directors of G. & J. Weir for a grand total of 164 years, during which the company's sales had grown from £116,000 to £16 million, and two major wars and the Great Depression had been survived.

These members of the founding family were not the only such long serving employees of the firm, although no one could equal Sir John Richmond, the last survivor of the handful of men who were there when the works at Cathcart was built. Another veteran was Jock Fox, the works chauffeur, who had accumulated no less than 62 years' service when he retired in 1954. Nor were the Weir and Lang families the only families at Weir's. Many families had worked at Weir's for three generations, and there were plenty of brothers there as well. Two brothers recalled with particular affection were the Leiths: Joe was foreman in the compressor shop, and Tom had a most distinguished career as a director of Weir Pumps.

In the 1950s there were no share option schemes, either savings-related ones for everyone or executive schemes for chosen senior personnel. Lord Weir and his brothers did however make an ex gratia transfer of shares to key employees, with an emphasis on those on the design side of the business.

When we compare that era with today one striking difference is in the company's degree of self-sufficiency. At the time when Weir's was established, its products, like most engineering companies of the day, were based on iron castings. A foundry was therefore an absolute necessity. (Indeed, the postal address of G. & J. Weir was Holm Foundry.) In any event, in late Victorian times, when inland transport still depended on a combination of rail and horse, it was pretty impractical to obtain components, particularly of any size or weight, from outside. Self-sufficiency went much further than that, though. In the 1950s Weir's had, apart from the more usual activities such as a smithy, welding shop, pattern shop and the like, facilities for the manufacture of components which today would certainly be bought in. For example, there was a small section which made pressure gauges, and another which turned out products as mundane as nuts, bolts and studs. There was also a gear

cutting department, and another making turbine blading.
Most unusual was the horse. He pulled a cart, but his most
vital function was supplying his regular by-product, which
was used for binding sand in the foundry.

In those days, before television arrived on a large scale,
with its impact (some would say a baleful one) on everyone's social life, there was a great number of leisure activities which revolved around the company. The recreation
grounds near the Cathcart works were excellent. The
bowling green was one of the best in the West of Scotland.
Tactfully, the local police were allowed to use it, thus
cementing good relations with the force. There were clubs
for tennis, football and cricket, and annual golf competi-
tions. There were also many other indoor activities with
particularly enthusiastic amateur dramatics. The drawing
office troupe rejoiced in the name of the 'Pencil Vainones'.
Television, and perhaps also increasing ownership of cars,
gradually led to declining interest in these communal pas-
times. In football, although Weir's Athletic won the Scottish
Amateur Cup in 1957 (in front of a crowd of 1,200 at
Hampden Park – probably the smallest-ever attendance at
that great stadium), only two of their team actually worked
at Cathcart. It was a change indeed from the wartime days,
when several members of the great Glasgow Rangers team
of that time had worked in the repair department. The
effect of television was not only confined to the employees.
Lord Weir became a television maniac in his retirement.
Unless he had more than two guests for dinner, he forsook
his dining room and ate dinner at a card table in the library
facing the television set. His butler crouched down as he
passed in front of the screen, so as not to obstruct his lordship's view. Conversation was sparse.

While the senior management of the firm were until
1954 mainly drawn from the founding Weir and Lang

families, almost all the middle and junior management had worked their way up in the company. There were few people recruited from outside. Although this resulted in a body of loyal people with great experience and knowledge of the company's products, it has to be said that it also led to a somewhat inward-looking culture and conservative attitude. On the technical side of the business also, men worked their way up from apprentice draughtsmen, improving their skill and knowledge through evening classes, mainly at the local technical colleges, where a number of senior Weir's employees lectured regularly. Hardly any graduate engineers were recruited.

But from 1954 onwards much was to change in the life of the firm.

4

Diversification and expansion

1954–72

After more than eighty years, G. & J. Weir found themselves facing pivotal changes in 1954. In that year, one whole generation of top management was succeeded by another. At the same time, the challenges to the business started to become more acute, and its leadership had to respond to these. We will see, therefore, how by various initiatives, some successful and some not, over the more than fifty years from 1954 to the present, they, and the management generations that followed them, reshaped the group into the form it has today. This chapter therefore covers the twenty years during which Kenneth Weir was chairman.

The situation which faced him and his colleagues when the older generation retired was not entirely favourable. True, the order book was a good one, and indeed, in spite of rising costs, profits before tax in 1955 and 1956 were only slightly less than the record of over £3 million for 1954. There were, however, two serious problems, one immediate and the other emerging.

The first of these, as has already been mentioned, had become an issue in the late 1940s and early 1950s. This was lack of capacity, in particular heavy machining capacity and assembly space.

This problem became acute with Weir's success in their land-based sea water evaporator business. In 1955 Weir's won a contract for a plant in Aruba, in the Netherlands Antilles, to produce 10,000 tons of fresh water per day; the contract was valued at £1.5 million. A few months later they won an equally large order to produce 4,000 tons of water per day and to supply power generation equipment for the neighbouring island of Curaçao. These plants incorporated a revolutionary system developed by Harold Hillier and Bruce Ling, Weir's technical director and chief chemist, which fed ferric chloride treatment chemical, produced from electrolytic cells, into the evaporators. As a result the plants were able to run continuously without any sea water scale forming, which had been the curse of sea water evaporators up to that time.

The individual evaporator units – five for Aruba and two for Curaçao – were of cast iron construction and extremely large. When pre-assembled at Cathcart, prior to dismantling them for shipment, each unit occupied an entire bay in the shops. The cast iron vessels were, in fact, made up of sections which were the largest castings that could be regularly obtained from British foundries, and which could only be machined by large machine tools. Accordingly Weir's looked around for suitable facilities which would at least ease the problem, and to this end purchased in 1956 William Simons & Co., shipbuilders and engineers at Renfrew on the Clyde, for a price of almost £600,000.

The founder of the business, William Simons, had had an unusual career. During the war of 1812 between Great Britain and the USA, he was asked by the Admiralty to go to Canada, where he constructed a number of warships for the naval conflict on the Great Lakes. They were excellent ships, but unfortunately all were sunk in action against the US Navy. Later on, Simons was responsible for supplying the whole of the iron framing which supported Joseph Paxton's celebrated Crystal Palace, originally built for the Great Exhibition of 1851 in Hyde Park.

Simons were not, however, conventional shipbuilders, but were makers of dredgers and other ships which had a high engineering content to them. When Weir's bought them, they had, as well as orders for dredgers, orders for two fish factory ships for Messrs Salvesen of Leith, and some special craft for the Admiralty – the strangely named paddle-wheel tugs *Griper* and *Grinder*, designed to manoeuvre aircraft carriers.

The fish factory ships, the *Fairtry II* and *Fairtry III*, were interesting and novel vessels. Their design was derived from Salvesens' experience in running one of the two British whaling expeditions. Like a whaling factory ship, they had a stern ramp up which the trawl net was hauled. The main catch was processed by automatic machinery into blocks of frozen fish fillets, which were sold under contract to hospitals, schools and prisons. The fish oil and other valuable residues were extracted and the waste made into fish meal.

The logic of the purchase, of course, depended not only on Simons helping to provide heavy machining capacity, but also continuing to be a profitable shipbuilder at the same time. Simons' machining equipment, however, was not very up to date, due to a lack of investment, and dredger building soon came under pressure from specialist Dutch shipyards who had the added advantage that most of the main dredging contractors, such as Blankenvoort, were based in Holland. Accordingly Weir's then purchased in 1958 Lobnitz and Co., another dredger specialist whose yard was next door to Simons, and who had a better machine shop. The firms were amalgamated as Simons-Lobnitz, with the hope that this would give sufficient cost savings to restore their competitive position in the dredger market.

During the Second World War, Lobnitz had played a key part in a very novel venture, the Mulberry Harbours. Until the Allies could capture a major port on the coast of northern France, they had to have some form of artificial harbour on the Normandy landing beaches so as to allow them to disembark men, equipment and supplies. Winston Churchill had said in a memorandum about the proposed artificial harbour, 'It must be able to go up and down with the tide.' It so happened that Lobnitz had a particular design of dredger which sank vertical columns into the sea bed, on which the dredger then rose and fell with the sea level. Lobnitz modified their system and ultimately constructed several of the modules which formed the Mulberry Harbour, although most of them were built to the Lobnitz design concept by other shipyards.

Ironically, however, the whole rationale of the Simons and Lobnitz purchases was fatally undermined by a revolutionary development by Weir's in sea water distillation. In 1955, Harold Hillier, Weir's technical director, died suddenly. Dr R. S. Silver was recruited in 1956 to replace him. Silver had worked before at Weir's, where he was in charge of research from 1939, but had left in 1946. Silver later recounted that when he first joined, the initial task J. G. Weir gave him was to look at Frank Whittle's gas turbine design and say 'if he thought it was sound'. Subsequently Weir's gave Whittle some modest financial backing, which Whittle (who had strongly socialist views about capitalist business) was very ungenerous in acknowledging. Weir's had never backed him to make a profit, and when Whittle's

Power Jets was nationalised, they put the proceeds into a ring-fenced fund to be used only for research.

Silver soon put in hand research that was to result in the multiple stage flash evaporator. At the time, the largest conventional evaporator units were limited, by the size of castings required, to an output of 250,000 gallons of fresh water per day each, and their efficiency (or performance ratio) to a maximum of around 4 to 1 in terms of the fresh water output relative to the heating steam supplied. To show how radical Silver's invention was, there are today single units producing 7 million gallons a day each, and performance ratios in excess of 10 have been achieved. The flash units moreover were steel fabrications, and the capital cost per gallon was far lower than for their predecessors. The pilot plant at Cathcart which demonstrated and proved the process and the associated research work all cost a mere £26,000, a modest figure for so significant a development. In a brave, if not foolhardy, move, the first unit sold commercially was twenty times the capacity of the pilot plant, and the second units – for Kuwait – were forty times its size.

The consequence of this was that very soon the heavy machining facilities at Simons-Lobnitz were no longer needed, and indeed fabrication of the new flash evaporators at the shipyards was soon seen to be uneconomic given the shipyard costs. A further blow was struck by the shipbuilding recession in 1958, which made the traditional business of Simons-Lobnitz heavily loss making. In 1961, therefore, Simons-Lobnitz was sold to the well-established Clyde shipbuilders Alexander Stephen. The whole episode therefore ended up as a failure, and a very expensive one at that.

As studies show, most acquisitions do not add value, at least to the acquirer, and with the benefit of hindsight, the lesson to be learned here was that Weir's did not make a good enough analysis of either the prospects of the core dredger business of the two companies or the inherent disadvantage of their poor cost structure as shipbuilders, even though they recognised that this very problem was already beginning to affect their established customers in the shape of UK yards generally.

The other part of Weir's capacity problem – the lack of assembly space – was connected, once again, to their iron foundry operations. As already recounted, the firm had partly addressed this in the 1920s with the formation of the Argus Foundry, although their foundry operation at Cathcart still continued. Cathcart did not have low costs, but was nevertheless very valuable in the decade after the Second World War, when outside supplies of castings were not only difficult to obtain, but also posed quality control problems. The Cathcart foundry also occupied a good deal of space on the site which could be put to better use as an up-to-date test shop and as an additional machine shop. It was accordingly decided in 1954 to move the entire foundry operation to the Argus site in Thornliebank nearby, and also incorporate equipment from the Coltness Foundry, which had been acquired a year or two earlier but then closed.

This move was not a success. Of course, it did ease the space problem at Cathcart, where an excellent test facility was then built, but the cost of the foundry investment ran very substantially over budget, and labour problems arose as a result of mixing the skilled foundrymen who were transferred from Cathcart, bringing their out-of-date working traditions and attitudes with them, with the mainly unskilled workforce at Argus. At the same time, not only did the management of the Argus operation clearly have shortcomings, but demand for iron castings of the lighter kind was in decline, while steel casting usage by Weir companies was increasing. Steel castings of good quality were moreover difficult to obtain.

The solution chosen was to purchase in 1958 a 50 per cent interest in Catton & Company, a leading steel foundry in Leeds, and put the Argus operations into a joint venture company with them, with S. L. Finch, the managing director of Catton's, in overall executive charge. In 1960 Weir's bought out the remaining 50 per cent share of the business and Catton's became a wholly owned subsidiary.

Not long after this, the iron foundry operations at Argus were closed, and Weir's foundry activities became concentrated on steel casting. The steel foundry business grew and was successful, until it eventually became the largest operation of its kind in the UK industry. In a sense, however, Weir's success in this area was more by accident than by design. The company initially entered the steel castings industry not because they saw merit and good commercial prospects in doing so, but principally to try to solve longstanding problems with their own iron foundries. To the company's credit, though, once they saw the potential of Catton's, they supported its success, and for the next twenty years, until the steel casting industry in turn faced severe problems of its own, steel foundry operations made a strong contribution to the group's results, despite at times being affected by cyclical demand and also requiring considerable capital investment.

So much for the first immediate problem that faced Kenneth Weir in 1954. The second was initially less pressing, but increasingly it became more serious, and that was the state of the marine market. The adverse factors here, which have been touched upon in earlier chapters, were two-fold. Steam power was increasingly giving way to diesel, which required far fewer Weir and Drysdale products. UK shipbuilding was rapidly losing the pre-eminent position it had occupied both in former times and even as late as the years immediately after the Second World War, and foreign shipyards were increasingly using domestic suppliers for the auxiliary machinery which was the basis of Weir's business. William Weir had forecast this development, albeit some ten years prematurely, in 1949, no doubt somewhat influenced by his experience in the period after the First World War. In any event, it was clear that radical action was needed to find new markets.

One important step had fortunately been taken in 1946, when Kenneth Weir became managing director. He had decided at that time to increase the firm's activity in supplying condensing and feed heating plant for the power station programmes both in the UK and overseas. This initiative, together with success in land-based sea water distillation plant, had worked well, and orders for land equipment, as distinct from marine, had formed an increasing part of the order book, exceeding 50 per cent in several years. Nevertheless, the inevitable decline in marine work required further determined action to make up the consequent shortfall of orders.

For a start it was decided to build on the existing compressor business. Although this was not a large business, the firm had since the early 1920s supplied starting compressors for diesel ships as well as special units (such as high-pressure torpedo-charging compressors) for the Royal Navy. Accordingly in 1959 a licence to manufacture reciprocating and centrifugal compressors for the process industries was acquired from Clarke Brothers of Olean in the USA. In 1960, a further step was the acquisition from Davy United of the Glasgow-based compressor maker Alley and McLellan Ltd. The Clarke deal, although it certainly provided shop load at a time when other work was short, was not really very satisfactory. The licence was simply for manufacturing, and sales were controlled by Clarke, who allocated manufacture to Weir's or to their own facilities or other licensees. No doubt at times the less attractively priced orders tended to go to Weir's, and not only were the prices that Weir's received affected by Clarke's substantial marketing expenses, but Weir's also had to pay high prices themselves for specialist components supplied by Clarke. Perhaps this assessment is debatable, but what was in no doubt was the high quality of Clarke's designs. Their integral gas engine driven reciprocating compressors were magnificent machines, which anyone would have been proud to build. Meanwhile, Alley compressors soon became an established part of the business at Cathcart, providing useful shop load at a reasonable profit margin.

One event in 1956, unrelated to the company's business, deserves special mention. That year was the centenary of the creation of the Victoria Cross. Naturally there was considerable press coverage of living holders of that famous award. As a result it emerged that Frederick Luke, who had worked for ten years as a storekeeper in the tool room at Cathcart, was, quite unbeknown to his workmates, a holder of the VC. On 26 August 1914, as a driver in the Royal Field Artillery, and aged only eighteen, he had gone back with three companions after their battery had been overrun by the Germans at Le Cateau, during the retreat from Mons, to try to recover the guns. He and his companions limbered up one gun and succeeded in bringing it back at full gallop and under heavy fire through the back of the advancing Germans. In 1919, shortly after the end of the war, and by then a sergeant, he had the additional distinction of being one of the small guard of honour at the burial of the Unknown Soldier.

In 1959 a further important commercial step was taken

with the acquisition of the French business ITAM (Société d'Installation Thermique et Auxiliaire des Machines), for a cost of £250,000. This was to prove an excellent investment in the long term. Not only did Weiritam, as the new business became known, provide growing profits over the years, but eventually Weir's interest in its successor company, Delas Weir, was sold for some £10 million. ITAM was an engineering company that primarily designed thermodynamic installations, but it did not manufacture them itself and instead subcontracted the work. It had been established by one Monsieur Marcheix, a brilliant engineer who was also most astute both commercially and financially. He had a small and very able young team, including in particular Michel Outin, who took over the management from him. ITAM specialised in condensing and feed heating plant, and in its early days also designed sugar refineries for customers such as St Louis and Béguin-Say. Before the Second World War ITAM had also been a formidable competitor of Weir's in the French marine market, and was involved in such prestigious vessels as the *Normandie* and later the *France*.

ITAM's greatest success was to come later, when Electricité de France embarked on its massive nuclear programme. Shortly after ITAM joined Weir's to became Weiritam, it expanded into Italy through the formation of SOWIT (Societa Weiritam SpA), which also was highly successful in the Italian power station programmes of ENEL and Edison Volta. Weiritam was a very cash-conscious operation, and not only made good profits on conventional contracting, but also made a banking profit by subcontracting its manufacturing on distinctly less favourable payment terms than those it received from its own customers. Incidentally, going to dinner with M. Marcheix was a notable experience. He favoured a small restaurant by the Seine, which specialised in gigot d'agneau carved vertically in small slivers, preceded by oysters fetched from a shop next door, and accompanied by Marcheix's own wine, which was kept at the restaurant. Nor was he immune in his younger days from other attractions. Before the war he and Harold Hillier, Weir's chief engineer, had found themselves in the same hotel in Italy, where they were competing for the same piece of business at the Ansaldo shipyard. In the evening, Hillier phoned Marcheix in a shocked state to say there was a young lady in his room, and asking how he was to get rid of her. 'I have one also: send yours along to my room if you are not interested' was the Gallic reply.

Weir's overall policy at that time was clearly reaffirmed by Kenneth Weir in the chairman's statement of 1961. It was:

1. To build up manufacturing load by new product development.
2. To enter process fields other than power.
3. To acquire interests in allied and associated undertakings, thus increasing the range of the Group's activities, and strengthening existing ones.

It was an ambitious programme, but one that was absolutely necessary. Needless to say, it had mixed results, with some successes and some failures, but radical action was necessary for the firm's survival, let alone its growth.

As the programme developed, it also produced managerial and organisational problems which had to be addressed. A start had been made some years earlier by the appointment of executive directors, in order to simplify the situation in which G. & J. Weir was not only the holding company but also an operating business in its own right. At the end of 1958, this was taken to its logical conclusion by forming G. & J. Weir Holdings Limited as the quoted parent company, and putting the Cathcart business into a separate operating company, G. & J. Weir Limited. At the same time, outside non-executive directors joined the holdings board. They were Sir Charles Connell, a leading shipbuilder; J. A. Lumsden, the company's lawyer; Sir Ian Stewart, chairman of Thermotank, the Glasgow industrial air conditioning and refrigeration firm; and John Lord, managing director of Dunlop. Kenneth Weir, shortly to succeed his father as 2nd Lord Weir, was chairman. John Drysdale was deputy chairman, and J. R. Lang and N. M. Niven were the executive directors, with J. J. B. Young in charge of finance.

Meantime further diversification of the Group continued. In 1961 Weir's, in conjunction with Booker Brothers McConnell, purchased the Pulsometer companies and divided them up. Weir's took the Pacific Pump licence and business (thus giving them an entry into the hydrocarbon process industry); BAL Polypac, a plastic and rubber hydraulic seal manufacturer; William Evans, who made reciprocating pumps; and Skihi, whose aircraft jacks expanded the range of Weir's subsidiary Zwicky, who supplied aircraft refuelling equipment. Although the Pacific Pump licence broadened Weir's product range, it was never wholly satisfactory. From a financial point of view the licence fees were high at 10 per cent of sales, and from a technical point of view the Pacific products were designed for US 60 cycle power rather than UK standards. Nevertheless the oil industry in those days was very conservative in its purchasing policy and never looked much further than Pacific, Byron Jackson, or United Pump designs.

These same considerations prevailed in the process industry market for valves, where the standard tended to be Crane, Walworth or Pacific designs. Weir Valves had originally been set up to meet capacity constraints at Cathcart and made light products, such as steam valves, for them. It had one early burst of prosperity with a large contract for atomic industry valves, but this had no continuing market, and Weir Valves struggled to develop a viable product line in steam valves against the strongly established competition of Hopkinson's and Dewrance. Accordingly a licence agreement was made with Pacific Valves of Long Beach, California, which gave Weir's, in return for a 25 per cent shareholding, not only a range of established process industry steel valves but also a developing range of ball valves. The latter were originally developed for service in the US space programme, but rapidly became widely used in many other applications. The name 'Weir Valves' was changed to 'Weir-Pacific Valves' as a result.

In the longer term Weir-Pacific was not a successful development. The basic problem was that the market for standard oil industry API cast steel valves was oversubscribed, with too many competitors in the UK and on the Continent, and price levels were weak for much of the time. Weir-Pacific was also not really well equipped with the right machine tools, and was too small and lacked experienced management. However, with specialist products it fared better. It was successful with low temperature cryogenic valves both for early liquid natural gas installations and for liquid oxygen service. It had good products for the whisky industry and parts of the food industry, and another excellent business in reactor valves once the British nuclear submarine programme got under way. It also had a small but profitable line in ultra high-pressure valves under licence from Autoclave, and a very good investment in Spain in Walthon-Weir Pacific. The latter was built up in Zaragoza by an outstanding entrepreneur, Sergio Piedrafita. Weir-Pacific took a 20 per cent interest when it employed only fifteen people, entirely because of their confidence in Piedrafita. In a very few years Walthon-Weir Pacific reached a turnover of £3 million, on which it made £1 million in pre-tax profit, and it was qualified worldwide as a supplier to Westinghouse and General Electric for Class 1 nuclear valves. With hindsight, Weir-Pacific should probably have operated on a much smaller scale and concentrated on specialist valves instead of also tackling the general valve market.

In 1961 a further diversification was undertaken with the purchase of the C. F. Taylor group of companies, based in Wokingham. Through Cierva, Weir's had a long-established interest in aviation. Both Lord Weir, as Secretary of State for Air in 1918 and subsequently with his heavy involvement in air rearmament in the 1930s, and J. G. Weir, as an early pilot and with his responsibility for aircraft procurement in both wars, were enthusiasts. The company had also manufactured aircraft during the First World War. The C. F. Taylor acquisition was therefore in a sense a re-entry into the aircraft industry, and also an expansion of Weir's existing if minor involvement through Zwicky's aircraft refuelling equipment. Underlying the acquisition, though, was a wider aim. Just as G. & J. Weir had made its way as suppliers of auxiliary equipment for the marine industry, so there was the ambition to do much the same in the aircraft industry through Taylor's.

The C. F. Taylor companies did however present some particular problems. They had been built up from nothing by Cyril Taylor, originally a skilled sheet metal worker by trade, and a man of much energy and ambition. His first great success was with the Vickers Viscount, the world's first turbo-prop airliner. Sales of this machine greatly exceeded Vickers' original expectations. The manufacturer was therefore forced to subcontract heavily and the C. F. Taylor group expanded rapidly on the back of this programme, supplying the jigs and fixtures on which the machines were built, and many component parts. They moved on from this into making precision fabrications for other aircraft and other manufacturers, and also turned their hands to a disparate range of other products, for many of which they were simply subcontract manufacturers. For example, they made Rotisamat chicken roasters (which you used to see in many supermarkets), Bake-O-Mat baking equipment and aircraft galleys, and they even marketed vacuum cleaners. Their most exotic, if small scale, product was breastplates for the Household Cavalry. They also had a subcontract design office where they undertook drawing office work on an hourly-rate basis for such projects as Concorde.

When Weir's bought Taylor's, they had to try and rationalise its whole structure. This was complicated by the fact that the company's finances and Mr Taylor's were confused to a considerable degree. Some of the company's more peripheral activities were disposed of, including two butcher's shops. (On being asked why he had these, Taylor's splendid answer was that he had two St Bernard dogs.) The business was soon put on a more rational and organised footing. The core business was good, and they executed some very demanding projects such as the ground flight testing installation for Concorde. Over the years the production of aircraft galleys became an increasingly important part of their activity.

Taylor's also had some bad luck which was not of their making. The Vanguard and the VC10 aircraft were as commercially unsuccessful as the Viscount had been successful. Most disappointing, however, was the failure during early flight testing of the first BAC111. At that point it was well ahead of any competitor and seemed likely to be a success on the same scale as the Viscount. As Taylor's were heavily involved, providing major fabrications such as the underbelly fairing and much else, they would have greatly prospered from this programme. The crash of the BAC111 prototype in October 1963 fatally delayed the programme and thus affected the level of sales, and BAC took much of the work back into their own facilities. Other planes, such as the Caravelle in France and the Douglas DC9 in the USA, were as a result able to catch up, and although the BAC111 eventually sold quite well, it never came near to matching the success of the Viscount.

With hindsight it is easy to see that there were parallels between Taylor's experience and Weir's experience with the shipbuilding industry. If you supply ancillary equipment to any industry, then your market is only as strong as that of your customer. The British aircraft industry was too fragmented after the Second World War and took too long to consolidate itself. In any event, at least on the civil aviation side, it was always going to struggle against US competition. Unlike the case of France, the industry was not helped by the inconsistency of British government policy and support. These were the roots of the problem for Taylor's, and although they tried manfully over the years, they could never fulfil Weir's over-optimistic expectations of growth and profitability.

In contrast with these diversifications, two minor product lines which had been entered into between the wars were dropped. One was industrial refrigeration, which had never been a great success financially, but which took up a disproportionate amount of space in the shops. The other was the manufacture of homogenisers, known colloquially as 'homos'. (No doubt in today's politically correct world this would be totally unacceptable and would have led to prosecution on some grounds or other.) Homogenisers were used for emulsification of products such as milk, ice cream and cosmetics, basically by pumping the substance at very high pressure through a valve where the constituent parts were broken up. Experiments were even carried out to study whether whisky could be artificially aged in this way, and naturally these were closely monitored by HM Customs and Excise. After the war, when there was food rationing, small ice cream makers were exempt, and many ice cream businesses sprang up, almost invariably owned by Scots of Italian origin. An embarrassing case to do with this arose when an elderly Italian lady appeared at Cathcart. She went to the sales department and ordered a small homogeniser on behalf of her family's firm. She carried a large paper bag, and absolutely insisted on paying for the machine in cash on the spot. Faced with this unusual approach, the Weir's administrative system failed. It was assumed that because the machine had been paid for, it had also been made and delivered. Months later, when the lady had still not received her homogeniser, a Latin drama of operatic proportions ensued. She was eventually given both a machine and her money back by way of apology.

Weir's concept of the flash evaporator had met early success in both Kuwait and Guernsey. In 1962 there was another important development in the desalination business. At around the time that R. S. Silver had been doing his pioneering work, Dr A. Frankel of Richardsons Westgarth was also working along similar lines. Not long after Weir's had built their first plants, Richardsons Westgarth entered the field and also won contracts. It did not seem sensible that there were two British firms both attacking the same market. Moreover, no sooner had Weir's got started than Japanese firms such as Ishikawajima Heavy Industries appeared as competitors, with virtually identical copies of Weir's design. Weir's did in fact have fundamental patents on the process, but unfortunately in the Arab countries which were the main market there was no patent law. An interesting attempt was made to establish whether the concept of a patent would be recognised in Koranic law. Eventually the leading authority, no less than the Grand Mufti of Cairo, gave the unsatisfactory opinion, at great length and in Arabic, that he did not really know. We will therefore perhaps never know whether theft of intellectual property can result in draconian penalties under Sharia law.

In 1962, Weir's and Richardsons Westgarth therefore combined their business as Weir Westgarth on a 50/50 basis, both of shareholding and the combination of personnel. This did not work well. The design philosophies of the two companies were somewhat different. The early Richardsons Westgarth plants experienced considerable difficulty in meeting required performance levels and consequently required extensive and costly modification, which occupied a lot of the management time of the new company. Both parents were at fault and violated the key rules of a jointly owned company, which are that you must not be partisan in favour of your former employees, you must respect the independence of the venture, either back or sack the management, and not interfere. After 1967, Weir's bought out Richardsons Westgarth, and Weir Westgarth became a wholly owned subsidiary under the management of A. C. Smith, formerly sales director at Cathcart.

The first major contract obtained by Weir's for the new multi-flash evaporators had been for a 500,000 gallon per day plant for the State of Guernsey. The Guernsey authorities ordered this to protect the island's important greenhouse tomato crop in case of water shortage. Their water engineer, a Mr Morgan, had carefully evaluated a desalination plant (knowing and indeed hoping it might never be used) against the alternatives of insurance at Lloyd's or building a reservoir. The plant attracted widespread publicity, and government recognition of the potential of this new development was demonstrated when it was opened by the Home Secretary, R. A. Butler. In fact the plant was used within a year or two and saved the day not only for tomatoes but also for tourists.

Guernsey was followed by two plants of one million gallons a day for the Government of Kuwait. Weir's agent in Kuwait called himself Sheikh Ezza Jaffir. In truth, and in spite of his impressive Arab dress and demeanour, he had started life as a boot boy in Shepherd's Hotel in Cairo, where he had caught the eye of a rich visiting Lebanese. The plant was erected by the Lebanese construction firm of Mothercat, a venture between Motherwell Bridge and Emile Bustani, the founder of CAT. Bustani had in his youth worked his way through Massachusetts Institute of Technology with his pay as a waiter. He was not only a most successful businessman and engineer, but also politically influential. He was sadly killed when his aircraft blew up outside Beirut harbour in 1963. It was strongly rumoured that it was sabotaged when he was on a peace negotiating mission.

On the steel foundry side, considerable development and expansion took place following the purchase in 1960 of a 100 per cent interest in Catton & Company. Investment was made in shell moulding facilities, and in 1962 E. Jopling and Sons in Sunderland was acquired. This company was engaged in a somewhat heavier end of the market than Catton, and therefore complemented it. Weir's was very satisfied with the progress and profitability of these steel foundry ventures, and therefore decided on a major initiative, to concentrate the Catton operations on a site at Knowesthorpe, outside Leeds, and construct a state-of-the-art foundry there. They planned this in conjunction with the consultants Knight Wegenstein, an offshoot of the

US engineers Lester B. Knight. The investment was planned to cost £2.35 million, and although there were significant cost overruns, and initial teething troubles commissioning the plant, eventually it was undoubtedly the best foundry in the UK. In reality it was three foundries in one. There was a new shell moulding line, where precision mass-produced smaller castings were turned out for such duties as tank tracks, valve parts, excavator teeth, and many other diverse services. Medium-sized products were made on a highly automated moulding line, and heavier products in a slinger section. Both carbon and stainless steel castings were produced, and excellent melting shop, testing, fettling and laboratory facilities put in.

In 1969 the opportunity arose to purchase for a modest price Osborn Hadfield Steel Founders in Sheffield. This was a combination of the steel foundry interests of Samuel Osborn and of Hadfield's, and it was losing money heavily. A very important asset was the licence from ESCO of Portland, Oregon. This was for castings of proprietary design which were used as standard components by equipment makers such as Caterpillar and their competitors for driving sprockets, excavator points, buckets and the like. One of Osborn Hadfield's specialities was manganese steel castings, much used in mining and earth-moving applications where heavy wear resistance was needed. After reorganisation and much-needed investment, the company quickly became profitable. The main works were in Sheffield itself, on the banks of the River Don. Hadfield's had a noteworthy history. Its founder, Sir Robert Hadfield, is credited with the invention of stainless steel and manganese steel in the 1880s. Indeed, manganese steel was often referred to as Hadfield steel. On a more frivolous historical note, the toilet and washing block at Hadfield's bore a plaque stating that 'these facilities were opened by William Ewart

James Weir,
co-founder of
G. & J. Weir, and
inventor of the
celebrated direct-
acting feed pump

A direct-acting
feed pump, Weir's
most famous
product

William Weir, later 1st Lord Weir, (at right) and his half-brother John Richmond, who was to become a discerning art collector, both in Darracq racing cars

Charles Ritchie working on the 130-mile Anglo Persian pipeline between Maiden-i-Naftun and Abadan

Early transport, *circa* 1910: a Serpollet–Darracq steam lorry used by Weir's, with a Weir air pump on the platform

In the works canteen, 1916: some of the 2,000 women in the Weir's workforce during the First World War

View of the turbine shop at the Cathcart plant, April 1930

A prototype Weir W-4 autogiro landing at Hounslow Heath in 1936

Second World War armaments: the gun cradle assembly
department, April 1942

August 1940: Australian gunners manning 25-pounder field
guns made by Weir's

King George VI and Queen Elizabeth visit the Cathcart plant in 1940

The 1st Lord Weir in the living room of a Weir-constructed Paragon house at Sighthill, Edinburgh, in July 1944. Paragon houses were built as council houses; the rent was 10 shillings a week. Lord and Lady Weir once stayed in one of them for two days to test their quality

Floor sections for prefabricated Weir houses being assembled
at the Weir Housing Corporation works at Coatbridge,
December 1947

The board of Weir's in 1956: (left to right) Sir Charles Connell;
J. W. Drysdale; J. G. Weir; N. M. Niven; John Spittal; J. J. B.
Young; John Davidson (company secretary); Kenneth Weir
(chairman); J. R. Lang; J. A. Lumsden

A familiar landmark: the clock tower at the Cathcart plant's
canteen and recreation centre in Newlands Road, on the south
side of Glasgow, in 1957

Gladstone, MP, Chancellor of the Exchequer'. You do not find Gordon Brown or Alistair Darling doing that sort of useful thing.

Osborn Hadfield's also had a subsidiary, Osborn Precision Castings, at Holbrook, outside Sheffield, later named Holbrook Precision Castings, or HPC. This was a very modern and excellent facility specialising in smaller alloy castings. It was a profitable business with a wide product range including roller seal rings for Caterpillar, which were turned out in tens of thousands, cutters for domestic kitchen grinders, stainless steel valve parts and even golf club heads. Over the years it was considerably expanded and improved. Both the timing and the cost of these acquisitions was awkward, however, as they coincided with heavy investment in commissioning the new foundry at Leeds.

Looking back, how should we judge Weir's involvement in steel foundries? They had excellent managers in Steve Finch and his deputy Alan Brearley, and for many years they made an important contribution to Group profits, although of course they were affected by the cyclical nature of the industry, and at times their export business suffered from exchange rate fluctuations. In the long term, however, steel foundries fell prey to much the same factors as had adversely affected both C. F. Taylor and Weir's original marine business. Their prosperity depended on the prosperity of their customers. In the case of the foundries, those customers made up most of the UK mechanical engineering industry. As that industry went into long-term decline, so did the prospects for steel casting, and the difficulty was compounded by the unwillingness of competitors to close down old plants with no chance of long-term profitability and thus reduce over-capacity in a declining market. The harsher critics might ask why Weir's made the mistake of being caught up in structurally declining markets not just once but three times, but to have avoided this would perhaps have needed a degree of long-term foresight denied to many, if not all, and in any event there were several years when the foundry profits made a vital contribution to Weir's overall results.

While these various developments went a long way towards meeting the strategic objectives which the chairman had set out in 1961, they did little towards strengthening Weir's activities in its important core activity of pumping. This part of the overall business was, in truth, not in good shape. In the early days of the company, although the direct acting steam driven pump had originally been introduced for boiler feed service, reciprocating pumps of this type had a much wider range of applications, for example in fuel oil service, early oil refineries, the sugar industry, gas works and much else. Over the years, however, they had been largely superseded by centrifugal pumps. This had of course been recognised by Weir's when they purchased Drysdale and Co. in the early 1920s. By the 1960s, however, Drysdale's faced much stronger competition, not only overseas, but also in the domestic market from competitors such as Worthington Simpson, Hamworthy Mather and Platt, Harland, W. H. Allen and others. (Hamworthy was actually founded by a ship owner, who considered Drysdale's products excessively expensive.) Drysdale's had a wide range of products, but apart perhaps from cargo-oil pumps for tankers, condenser circulating water and condensate extraction pumps, and the dry-dock dewatering service, it was not a market leader and produced too many lines on too small a scale. At Cathcart itself, apart from the Pacific Pump products, the pump business mainly comprised boiler feed pumps for power stations and specialist marine pumps for the naval market and merchant steam ships. The latter market became increasingly difficult from 1960 onwards, as British shipyards lost their place to foreign competitors using local auxiliary machinery. There were moreover several strong competitors in the boiler feed pump market itself, and, at least in the early 1960s, Weir's designs were neither very advanced nor very competitive in price or performance.

It can of course be argued with hindsight that if diversification was needed – as it clearly was – it did not necessarily mean entering new fields such as aircraft equipment or steel foundries as was in fact done. It could equally have been achieved simply by concentrating on a major expansion, whether by acquisition or product development, in the pump industry itself. Indeed, in a real sense pumps are by their nature themselves a diversified product, as their applications are so varied and cover such a wide range of different markets. Another effect of relying less on any individual market is that the cyclical effects on demand from a wide range of customer industries are less likely to coincide.

This proposition, however, although logically correct, would only have been valid and practical if good opportunities for putting it into effect had been available, and if there had also been sufficient financial resources to do so. Weir's started to take action to address the first point in 1965. The company's financial resources were in fact heavily devoted to the combined costs incurred in buying Simons-Lobnitz and funding their subsequent losses; in the purchase of the C. F. Taylor aircraft equipment business; and in the purchase of and very heavy subsequent capital investment in steel foundries. The resources that went into these costs could otherwise have funded major expansion in pumps. Whether Weir's overall results would have been better if the company had concentrated instead on the pump business is difficult to say, but they might not have become as over-stretched financially as was later to become the case.

In the event, in 1965 it was decided to approach the firms of Mather and Platt in Manchester and W. H. Allen in Bedford to see whether the pumping interest of the three firms could somehow be combined. Mather and Platt were a long-established centrifugal pump maker. Indeed their first machines had been designed by Professor Reynolds of Manchester University, a pioneer of hydraulic theory. They were a strong and direct competitor of Weir's in boiler feed pumps, and well established in the water industry. Allen's competed with Drysdale's in large cooling water pumps and similar applications. The chairmen of the companies all knew each other well, and initially the concept was received with considerable enthusiasm, but when detailed negotiations, led by J. W. Atwell, the managing director of Cathcart, got under way in 1966, two problems emerged. The first was the practical difficulty of disentangling pump operations from the numerous other activities which each of the companies carried on. Much more fundamental, however, was the question of the relative shareholding of each company in the new business. On comparisons of assets, sales, and profitability, Weir's were clearly entitled to majority control. The others would not accept this, and after two years the proposed venture collapsed. Ironically, many years later Weir's acquired both Allen's and Mather and Platt's pump activities for modest sums. For the moment, however, Weir's found themselves in 1967 back where they had started.

They then turned their attention to the possibility of acquiring the Harland Engineering Co., who were based at Alloa in Scotland but also had overseas interests in South Africa, Australia and Canada. Harland were direct competitors of Weir's in boiler feed pumps, but also had a wide range of pumps for markets Weir's did not cover effectively, and in addition manufactured electric motors, paper mill drive systems, and hydro-electric turbines. Their technology was good and they clearly offered a good fit with Weir's. Early in 1968, the possibility of acquiring Harland was greatly enhanced when Weir's were approached, through Parsons and Co., the Glasgow stockbrokers, with an offer to sell them a 15 per cent shareholding in Harland which was owned by Northern Engineering Industries. Weir's bought these shares and, with subsequent purchases in the market, soon held an 18 per cent interest in Harland.

In November 1968, a formal offer was made for Harland. In those days the Industrial Reorganisation Corporation had been set up by the Wilson Government with wide ambitions to promote consolidation in British industry. Weir's initiative was not at all to the corporation's taste, and they wanted Harland and Mather and Platt to be combined. Roger Brooke, the chief executive of the IRC, immediately (and somewhat improperly) told Weir's they would fight the proposal, and was given an appropriately rude reply. A takeover fight then ensued, with Mather's counter-bidding for Harland. Weir's were advised by Sir Walter Salomon of Rea Brothers, by Rowe and Pitman, and by Martin Lampard of Ashurst Morris Crisp, who was probably the best corporate finance lawyer in the City. It could fairly be said of the latter that he enjoyed life to the full, and there was some feeling that his advice was sometimes better before lunch than afterwards. Walter Salomon was a unique character. In the 1930s he had come to London from Hamburg as a refugee from Hitler (as had other notable German financiers such as S. G. Warburg), and after a time had purchased Rea Brothers, a small bank originally established in Liverpool. He was a stout advocate of private enterprise and described himself as a Gladstonian Liberal. Although he wrote excellent and stylish English, the same could not always be said of his command of the spoken word, particularly when excited. Among his memorable phrases uttered with a distinct German accent were, 'It goes off my back like duck's water,' and 'He wants to have his cake and sit on it.'

In the end Weir's won, and Harland's was acquired in January 1969. Weir's had the considerable advantage of owning at the start almost 20 per cent of the Harland shares, which had been bought at little more than half the price at which the acquisition was eventually made. Takeover bids often result in hard feelings, but in Harland's case their managing director, Kenneth Atchley, and his very able deputy, Ludwig Spiro, accepted what had happened in a most gentlemanly and generous way, and both played important ongoing roles with Weir's. The acquisition of Harland's brought with it Harold Anderson, an excellent designer who played an important role, together with George Arkless of Weir's, in improving the company's product line.

This was one of the most important acquisitions Weir's ever made. It put them in the position of being the leading UK pump maker, and provided the basis on which they were able to build before emerging eventually in the pre-eminent position they occupy today in the industry.

However, although the Harland's acquisition greatly improved and widened Weir's product range, and incidentally reduced competition in some areas, there was still an important gap in the standard mass-produced pump market. Here the leader was Worthington Simpson in Newark. Accordingly Weir's attempted to acquire Worthington Simpson also, making an offer in December 1968, when they were already confident that the bid for Harland's would be successful.

This initiative was a bold one, particularly as Studebaker-Worthington of the USA, who owned 10 per cent of Worthington Simpson, were a very large concern and indeed had already made an offer for the company. Worthington's was an ancient competitor to Weir's. Henry Worthington had developed a feed pump for river and canal steam boats in the USA at the same time as James Weir developed his boiler feed pump. Worthington was not only an excellent engineer, but a ruthless and astute businessman who eventually succeeded in forming the Pump Trust in the USA, which became the subject of notorious anti-trust action. As already recounted, the 1st Lord Weir had missed the opportunity of acquiring control of Worthington's in 1938. Studebaker-Worthington had been formed by Derald Ruttenberg, a brilliant entrepreneur and businessman. He had bought the Studebaker car company when it was on its knees. No one thought you could close down an automobile maker with all its ongoing liabilities, such as warranties to its dealers and union commitments, without going bust. Ruttenberg succeeded, however, and was then left with the valuable non-automobile interests of Studebaker – such as Onan generators and STP engine additives – and a very large tax loss. He merged with Worthington's, which was thought to be a steady profit earner, with the intention that Worthington's profits and those of the other operations would then become tax free, with evident benefit to the net earnings per share of Studebaker-Worthington.

The Industrial Reorganisation Corporation, who had by now swallowed their chagrin at Weir's takeover of Harland's, then intervened and proposed that Weir's and Studebaker-Worthington should try and reach an agreed solution, failing which the IRC would adjudicate between them and decide the winner. After prolonged negotiations it was agreed that Weir's would withdraw their offer, and in return a substantial part of the Worthington product line would be manufactured by Weir's at Cathcart for assembly and test in a jointly owned facility to be set up in the USA near Baltimore. Weir's would, however, still be able to compete in the standard pump business. This was not really logical, and a few months later it was agreed that Weir's would acquire 50 per cent of Worthington Simpson in return for taking on the liability of a 10-year loan of 55 million deutschmarks. At times the chairman of Studebaker-Worthington, Bob Guthrie, took part in the negotiations himself. Guthrie was a Southerner, and was senior partner in the law firm of Nixon, Guthrie, Mudge and Mitchell. Two of his partners had rather differing and unusual careers. Nixon became US President. Mitchell became his Attorney General and ended in jail.

Shortly after the Studebaker-Worthington transaction was completed, G. & J. Weir Ltd., Drysdale's and Harland's were amalgamated to form Weir Pumps in 1969, and a programme of rationalisation was put in hand, which included the closure of Harland's facility for manufacturing small pumps at Timperley in Cheshire and subsequently Drysdale's plant at Yoker.

In desalination the early successes of Weir's in Kuwait and Guernsey and of Richardsons Westgarth in Qatar and Curaçao were followed up by Weir Westgarth winning in 1963 a contract in Kuwait for five plants, each with a capacity of one million gallons a day. There was intense competition from Westinghouse for this contract, and the Weir Westgarth offer had a price advantage of only half a per cent. The reaction of the Kuwaiti agent of Westinghouse was hysterical. At the bid opening he shouted, 'You are Weir pigs,' – a notable Islamic insult – 'you live by bribes!' Thereafter Westinghouse withdrew from the business.

Shortly before that Weir's had to face a serious setback, though. At the time when Dr Silver had first developed the multi-flash system, Weir's had bid for two large plants for the Bahamas Electricity Corporation. Unfortunately the then technical director at Weir's lost his nerve and persuaded the management not to offer the new flash system but instead to supply a mongrel design made of a stainless steel clad construction and combining in a complex manner some elements of flash evaporation with conventional submerged tube technology. Not only were there serious difficulties in physically assembling the structure, but once that was achieved the process design was a total failure and the plants could hardly produce more than 50 per cent of rated output. Accordingly the brave but extremely expensive decision was taken to scrap the plants and replace them with multi-flash units, which were built for Weir's by the Chicago Bridge and Iron Company in the USA. The disastrous episode cost Weir's nearly £1 million, although they earned considerable admiration for the way in which they had stood behind their commitments to their client.

The success of Weir Westgarth and the wide publicity given to the emergence of large-scale desalination and its long-term potential led to intense competition as several large companies took advantage of the lack of patent protection in Arab countries and enthusiastically entered the field. The Japanese firm of Ishikawajima Heavy Industries was the first to do so with a precise copy of Weir's original design for Kuwait, which even included some detailed design errors Weir's had made. Ishikawajima were followed by Mitsubishi and Hitachi, Alsthom and Sidem in France, several Italian firms, and others. None of these companies had any background or experience in the technology, which required not only sophisticated thermodynamics and hydraulics, but also an in-depth understanding of the chemistry of sea water and the associated problems of avoidance of corrosion and scale formation. They were all seduced by the long-term potential of desalination, and in several cases were supported financially and politically by their governments. The obvious result was severe competition, and for Weir Westgarth a lean period ensued, with few major orders until 1968, when important orders were won for Abu Dhabi and the island of Jersey.

The first small desalination plant had been supplied to Abu Dhabi around 1960. At that time Abu Dhabi had not yet benefited from large oil revenues. It was still quite primitive and business conditions there were unusual. The Ruler was Sheikh Shakhbut, who was a traditionalist and, to say the least, not very attuned to Western ways. He stored part of the initial cash payment made by the oil companies in the cellars of his fort. Considerable complications arose when much of it was eaten by rats. His family had ruled for many generations, and apparently he was anxious to die in bed, something which many of his forebears had failed to do, instead meeting violent ends. This ambition was greatly assisted when the British Government – as part of the policy of withdrawing from east of Suez – had him exiled and replaced by his younger brother.

The ruling family were, like many Arabs, keen falconers. Accordingly Weir's promised one of them a picture of a white Arctic Falcon which Douglas Weir, my younger brother and a noted ornithologist, was going to paint. Alas, there was a misunderstanding, and it transpired that it was a real, live bird that was expected, not just a painting of one. Rising to the challenge, Weir's obtained, at great difficulty and expense, a specimen of this very rare bird from a gamekeeper in Bohemia who had caught one during migration. Due to its cost, it was decided to insure it. Stenhouse, the insurance brokers, found an underwriter in Lloyd's who was a birdman, and duly obtained a policy which bore the notation 'subject to being fed at intervals a mouse, a rat, a mole, or a vole as roughage'. A photo of the bird was required. Shamefully, this was provided by the subterfuge of copying a photo from a bird book. At any rate the bird was gratefully received alive and well in Abu Dhabi, having travelled by British Airways in a first class seat of its own. The munificence of this present can be measured by the fact that King Richard I of England was ransomed in the crusades for a pair of white falcons. Abu Dhabi shortly afterwards awarded a major desalination contract to the Japanese on a price difference of half a per cent, but to Weir's satisfaction the Japanese plant performed very poorly.

One contract worth a mention, due to its peculiar outcome, was the supply of a 500,000 gallon per day plant to the Sinai Manganese Company in Egypt. It was part of a project consisting of a manganese smelter, a gas turbine power station and a desalination plant. The smelter was provided by the Norwegian firm Electrokemist, whose chief engineer rejoiced in the unlikely but highly appropriate name of Knut Sandbolt, and the power plant was supplied by Brown Boveri in Switzerland. The plant was duly built and financed by letters of credit over a ten-year period and denominated in Swiss francs. Alas, before the installation could be commissioned the Israelis invaded Sinai and promptly took the plant to bits and shipped it off to the town of Eilath, where they re-erected it. They then had the nerve to ask for a commissioning engineer to be sent out. Weir's however answered that they did not commission stolen property. Meanwhile, as time went on, Weir every year cashed a letter of credit. This had a fortunate outcome for them, as almost every year the Swiss franc rose against sterling.

From 1968 to 1972 there was again a dearth of orders for major plants, and the staff at Weir Westgarth had to be cut back severely. It was also decided that, in view of the success of Japanese firms, a major company in Japan should be licensed. After tortuous negotiations – mainly caused by the traditional Japanese requirement of unanimity and internal consensus – a licence agreement for fifteen years was signed with Sumitomo Heavy Industries. Apparently thirteen people had to agree. There was one odd man out, but luckily he retired. This not only earned some royalties, but also gave Weir Westgarth access to Sumitomo's excellent and efficient fabrication facilities.

In 1972, however, the tide turned again with a large further order from Abu Dhabi. Competition remained intense, and was exacerbated by two factors. First, most Arab governments awarded contracts almost entirely on the basis of the lowest price, and with little regard to the experience or competence of the suppliers. Second, the consulting engineers they engaged were also chosen simply on price, regardless of the fact that desalination was such a specialised field. It was rather like someone who needed brain surgery putting the operation out to tender and giving the job to the cheapest surgeon. Some of the political interference, notably by the French, was particularly odious.

These comments are in no way sour grapes, however. The truth is that Weir Westgarth plants did perform outstandingly well. For example, a plant supplied to the Kuwait Oil Co. at Ahmedi in 1962 ran from the moment it was started up for over 300 days continuously at above its rated output, and was then shut down only for a day or two because the seal on a pump was leaking. For any process plant, that was a terrific record. Nevertheless, there was little customer recognition of performance of that class. Somehow in the Middle Eastern psyche there seemed to be no concept of the difference between value and price. Much of the credit for Weir Westgarth's performance must go to Andrew Smith, previously the sales director at Cath-cart. He came from Rothesay on the Island of Bute, and was a long-serving member of the company, having started as an apprentice in the 1930s at a time when trade was so poor that apprentices worked two weeks on and two weeks off. He was a most excellent salesman, and combined charm with ability to an exceptional degree.

In 1967 it was decided to extend Weir's reach in the water industry, and to try to compensate for the erratic per-formance of Weir Westgarth, who from the nature of their contracts went from feast to famine. Accordingly the water treatment firm of William Boby, in Rickmansworth, was bought. Boby covered industrial water treatment, including plants for power stations, and had a good and solid reputa-tion. To it were added the small existing businesses of Weir Water Treatment and G. S. Tett, who were mainly engaged in water softening installations. After a few years, however, it was decided that Weir's could not support both desalina-tion and conventional water treatment on the scale required, and Boby was sold to the Permutit company.

The story of Weir Housing – later to be renamed Weir Construction in 1970 – during the period from 1954 was an interesting and varied one. The driving spirit of the company was Arthur Cargill. When Weir Housing was first set up, Lord Weir recruited Cargill by the simple expedient of driving around Scotland and looking at various local authority housing schemes. The best ones seemed to him to be in Dumfries, so he hired their architect. Weir Housing initially concentrated on the local authority housing market. Naturally this meant it was subject to a considerable degree to the vagaries of government policy in this field. Not only was the company therefore affected by the number of houses that government decided should be built, but the degree to which individual local authorities accepted Weir's concept of industrialised manufacture, and particularly of standardised components, was also a serious issue. It could reasonably be said that whereas Weir Housing logically and rationally saw the benefit to all of standardised low-cost factory-produced house components, unfortunately a considerable number of their local authority customers did not. Often a crucial factor was that local authorities had their own architects, who, with all due respect, were not leading members of their profession, but nevertheless had the professional ambition to make their own mark on the houses for which their authority was responsible. Clearly there was a distinct dilemma between the two positions.

Weir Housing's position was further complicated by the forthright views, when it was first set up after the war, of Lord Weir, who had strong prejudices against dealing with Glasgow Corporation, who were obviously a very important potential customer. To put it politely, he did not think that, at that time, Labour administrations in Glasgow necessarily had quite the same commercial integrity that he had. Accordingly, apart from, on occasion, taking components and some timber bungalows, they were not a customer. In spite of all this, however, over a long period when local authority housing in Scotland as a whole ran at around 30,000 houses per year, Weir's had a fairly consistent share of around 10 per cent, or 3,000 units a year. That was not a bad effort for a group who were really mechanical engineers.

Certainly Weir Housing was a good contributor to overall profits for much of the period from 1954. In some years, for example when they had a large contract for all-timber houses, which exactly fitted their production system, they made exemplary returns. In their earlier years, they had little competition from outside Scotland, for example from the major English firms such as Wimpey and Costain. When the local authority market in England turned down, as it did toward the end of the 1960s, these firms turned their attention to Scotland, and competition greatly increased.

In 1967 Weir Housing made what, with hindsight, was a serious mistake. Trusting, as has already been said, to the logic of their view that the future lay in standardised factory produced house components, they greatly expanded their facilities at Coatbridge and took on significant loan commitments as a consequence. This expansion increased their operational gearing, and by 1970, when demand had not increased as anticipated, and more competition came into Scotland, it had serious repercussions. Several years before that, they had first entered the private housing market. This was not, however, on a very large scale, and the private market was not by its nature a market very compatible with their expertise, which always lay in mass produced components. Moreover they really did not have the particular expertise needed for large-scale property development and private housing schemes, even although they had a excellent sales director in Gordon Murray. Private housing was therefore not on a scale to compensate for the difficulties in the public housing market. The result was heavy losses of £470,000 in 1970, and £250,000 in 1971.

The verdict therefore has to be that, although for more than twenty years Weir Housing had been a success, and even in several years a substantial contributor to the overall profits of the Group, in the end, through a combination of increased competition and the strategic misjudgement which resulted in overinvestment in its production facilities, it became a liability to Weir's. Moreover, on the way to reaching that unfortunate position, it had added considerably to the liabilities of the company as a whole. This is easy to say with hindsight. No one remembers today, when looking at many new housing schemes in the private or public sector, that the way houses are built now was first pioneered by Weir's. (But then again, Christopher Columbus discovered America and never made a dollar out of it.) Eventually, in 1974 Weir Housing (by now renamed Weir Construction) was sold to the firm of Ernest Ireland. Unfortunately Irelands went bust eighteen months later, after paying only 50 per cent of the selling price.

As for foundries and engineering supplies – the latter represented by Polypac BAL – we have so far mainly considered the acquisitions which were made and the heavy investment programmes which followed them. In looking at the contribution made by the steel foundries, it is important to understand that they operated in an industry where demand was strongly cyclical in nature. During the period covered by this chapter, that contribution to Group profits was a very important one. It was also greatly to the credit of their management that, even in years when low demand created serious problems for their industry as a whole, they almost invariably performed better than the competition. The management's performance was supported by the investment that had been made in excellent facilities. It was only in the late 1970s that decline in their customer base produced more intractable problems. In engineering supplies, Polypac BAL produced excellent results for several years following its acquisition. Problems there emerged only when it was moved from Halesowen in the Black Country to a new and ambitiously expanded plant in Hartlepool under untried management. Its offshoot in Italy, Polypac SpA, in comparison consistently produced excellent results and strong growth.

In 1954 the only overseas activity of Weir's of any consequence was its involvement in Peacock Brothers in Montreal. Weir's had been a shareholder since before the Second World War. During the war, Peacock's operations expanded considerably, and as a Weir licensee they built much equipment for the Royal Canadian Navy, which played a major role in the Battle of the Atlantic, supported by a large-scale warship construction programme at Canadian shipyards. Weir's bought out the other British minority shareholders, who included Hopkinson's, but Peacock's continued to be the sales agent for Hopkinson's valves which had a wide acceptance in the Canadian power industry. As a result Weir's then became majority shareholders in 1957. In the period after the war, the gap in demand was increasingly filled by manufacture of the well-known Nordstrom tapered plug-cock valve, which was used worldwide in the natural gas and oil industry. This industry developed rapidly in Canada with the discovery and exploitation of massive finds of gas (and oil) in Alberta.

By 1961, a new plant had been built exclusively for valve production at Highland Park in Montreal, and Nordstrom by this time had a one-third shareholding in Peacock's. Nordstrom was acquired by Rockwell, a major American corporation involved in the automotive industry, and subsequently in aviation and defence. Rockwell also had a large power station valve business, Edward Valve, and wished to have all the valve operations under their direct control. Accordingly Weir's sold Peacock's Nordstrom valve business to Rockwell and in turn bought out Rockwell's shareholding in Peacock's in 1961. In the short term this was an attractive proposition financially, but it did leave a large hole in Peacock's manufacturing load.

Peacock's were unfortunately not at all successful in filling this gap, and were consistently unprofitable until Jim Crowdy – a mining engineer, and Kenneth Weir's brother-in-law – became president in 1965. Thereafter they rightly concentrated on building up their service activities across Canada and increasing their sales agency business in tandem.

Peacock's position improved considerably after Weir's acquisition of Harland's, whose Canadian activities were combined with their own. This also brought in J. A. Cumming, who managed Harland's Canadian business and who made a great contribution to their ultimate success. New service centres were established in Edmonton and then Calgary, and in the 1970s the company's headquarters was transferred from Montreal to Toronto in reaction to the growth of separatist sentiment in Quebec. After a year or two, Peacock's returned to profit, and made a useful contribution to the overall results of the Group.

During most of the period from 1954 to 1972, the main factor determining the overall results of the company was the performance of G. & J. Weir at Cathcart and, to an important but lesser extent, that of Drysdale's at Yoker. Until around 1960, the housing activities provided an additional and at times major contribution. From that point onwards, with the exception of one or two years of recovery, earnings from housing went into a declining trend, eventually turning into losses and finally leading to the disposal of that operation. After 1960, however, the steel foundries started to contribute to the results, and as they expanded from a combination of acquisition and investment they contributed on an increasing and important scale.

The management at Cathcart and Yoker changed considerably during this period, in terms of both structure and people. In 1954, executive directors solely responsible for operations at Cathcart were appointed. In 1958, as we have seen, G. & J. Weir Holdings was formed and the business at Cathcart became a subsidiary as G. & J. Weir Limited. (Only in 1967 was the holding company renamed The Weir Group.) Kenneth Weir remained for a short period chairman at Cathcart, as well as at the holding company, with

J. R. Lang as managing director, J. W. Atwell as his deputy, and J. J. B. Young, A. C. Smith, R. S. Silver and G. Milligan responsible for the finance, sales, technical and production functions respectively.

At this point, Guy Milligan deserves special mention. He had started at Weir's as a young labourer but transferred to being an apprentice, which was most unusual, and worked his way up, eventually becoming managing director at Cathcart. He was an excellent manager and was held in great affection by all. Much of his time was spent as manager of the repairs department. Apart from carrying out repairs to customers' machinery in the shops at Cathcart and providing spare parts, the repair department also employed the 'outside squad'. This squad was something of an elite, and their functions not only included work on equipment at customers' sites, but also commissioning machinery (particularly on trial trips of new ships) and the start-up of power stations. Notable members of the squad were Willie Hill, Andy Stevens, Joe Copeland, 'Baldy' Simpson and John Pollock. Baldy was known to lose his head sometimes at moments of stress. On one trial trip of a new ship he was heard to shout at the apprentice with him, 'Up that ladder quick and shut that valve.' Up the lad went. 'It's shut, Baldy.' 'Well, open it then!' When working at John Brown's, he was known to enjoy what he called 'a hydraulic lunch' in the Admiralty Bar outside the shipyard gates. This consisted of mince on a piece of toast (price sixpence) washed down with two pints of Aitkens Heavy, a beer advertised by the picture of a tiger, and the slogan 'Strength behind bars'. They were a great bunch of people.

In 1961, J. R. Lang took over from Kenneth Weir as chairman at Cathcart. J. W. Atwell succeeded Lang as managing director and held that post until 1968, when a formal divisional structure was adopted and he took over responsibility for the Engineering Division as its chairman. At Drysdale's, N. M. Niven and John Young were joint managing directors until John Drysdale retired in 1962, when Niven took over as chairman, with John Carpenter as managing director.

Until about 1960 both Cathcart and Drysdale's prospered, thanks to a buoyant market for merchant shipbuilding, particularly oil tankers, and solid demand for naval vessels. The land market was also strong, with a large power station programme both in the UK and overseas. The next three years were difficult for both companies, resulting from increased competition and a drop in demand, not only causing output to fall, but also putting profits under pressure as the margins fell on such new business as was booked. Thereafter Cathcart's earnings recovered, although they did not reach previous peaks, at least in real terms. Drysdale's continued to have difficult times.

There were, however, many notable achievements during the period. Drysdale's had particular success in dry dock dewatering pumps based on their excellent patented 'Syphonic' system and, in the earlier part of the period, they supplied a great number of cargo oil pumps to the tanker market. In many cases these were driven by Weir steam turbines built at Cathcart. A new heavy machine shop was installed at Yoker in 1955. This enabled Drysdale's to meet the demand from the power station programme for increasingly large condenser circulating pumps. They supported this particular market with an excellent hydraulics facility for modelling the flow of water at power station inlets. In 1958, for example, they won the order for six 72-inch circulating pumps for Hinckley Point nuclear power station, which at that time were the largest such pumps made. In the water supply industry, another interesting contract for

Drysdale's was for the pumping station to bring water from the island of Lantau to Hong Kong.

Cathcart had its highlights too. In 1956 the contract was won for the condensing and feed heating plant and the boiler feed pumps for the experimental reactor at Dounreay in north-east Scotland. In the same year they were awarded the contract for the reactor circulating pump for the land-based prototype of the nuclear submarine *Dreadnought*, appropriately bearing the same name as the battleship which had revolutionised naval warfare early in the century. This led to the development, of the reactor pumps for succeeding generations of nuclear submarines for the Royal Navy. A specialist clean-room facility was built in Cathcart for the assembly and testing of these machines, under conditions similar to a hospital operating theatre.

As the civil nuclear programme got under way, Cathcart had numerous other successes, for example supplying the feed pumps for three of the four stations ordered in 1957 – Berkeley, Hunterston and Hinckley Point. Orders also followed for condensing and feed heating plant at other nuclear stations. In 1959 they received the contract for the feed pumps for Thorpe Marsh coal fired station. The main pump which handled 4 million pounds per hour of feed water at 485 degrees Fahrenheit, and had a discharge pressure of 2,800 pounds per square inch, was at the time the largest machine ordered in the world. Over the years, further major orders were won, particularly large ones being feed pumps for Ferrybridge and Drakelow power stations, and condensing and feed heating plant for the South of Scotland Electricity Board at Cockenzie and Kincardine.

Two problems highlighted by Kenneth Weir were to have future repercussions. First, the formation of GEC by Arnold Weinstock meant that the power plant interests of AEI, Metro Vick, GEC and English Electric were amalgamated. All of these except GEC were suppliers of their own heat exchange equipment, as was C. A. Parsons, the other turbine maker. As a result, Weir's were effectively cut out of the condensing and feed heating market in England, and confined to Scotland, where the SSEB's practice was to order this equipment separately from the main generating plant. Eventually this limitation was to make the market unviable for Weir's.

The second problem was that as turbo-generators got larger, reaching 600 megawatts individually, so the number of stations got smaller, and as a consequence larger but fewer feed pumps were needed. As there were three British makers, Weir's, Mather and Platt, and Harland, and the Swiss firm of Sulzer was also entering the UK market, consolidation in the industry was clearly desirable, and this was an important factor behind the acquisition of Harland and the eventual purchase of Mather and Platt's pump business.

One other event cannot pass without remark. In 1959 the desalination plants in Aruba and Curaçao, the last major units to be manufactured at Cathcart, were commissioned. In Aruba the opening was marked by the issue of a special postage stamp depicting them. At the same time the Amstel brewery in Curaçao (not the parent business in Holland) won the best beer competition at the Brussels Exhibition. The managing director of the parent attributed this, quite rightly, to the excellent quality of water which Weir's plant provided. Indeed, Bill Vandersteel, Weir's agent in New York, reached the point of persuading the managing director that the labels of the beer bottles would carry the legend 'brewed with Weirwater'. Alas, the Amstel man retired before this splendid advertisement for Weir's was put into effect. However, the bathrooms of the hotels in the two islands carried for a time stickers reading, 'Weirwater, distilled from the sea; purer than rain; better than nature's best; use it freely but sparingly.' In today's age of the bottled water craze, what an early commercial opportunity Weir's missed.

Incidentally, once piped water was laid on to the villages in Aruba it was only available at first from public taps, and unfortunately these were at times left running. The problem of wasting this precious resource was solved by a lady in Mr Vandersteel's office in New York. She suggested delicately that the solution was to be found in a piece of equipment in gents' rest rooms called the Sloan Royal Flushcock, which was a spring-loaded valve which shut itself off after releasing a limited amount of water. Another triumph of technology.

During the period covered by this chapter the overall results of the Group were erratic. Certainly they did not show the sort of steady progression in profits which share-holders would have liked. From 1954 onwards, there were three distinct phases. For the five years to 1960, profits before tax averaged around £2.5 million. There was no debt, and indeed net cash increased from £1 million in 1954 to over £3 million by 1959. During these five years the pretax return on capital employed fell, however. In 1954 it had been 27 per cent, but by 1958 it had declined to 11.5 per cent, although this was still quite respectable by indus-try standards. (For example, Hopkinson's, the valve maker who served many of the same customers, made a return on capital of just 10.5 per cent in 1958.) Adjusted for inflation, though, profits in real terms declined considerably more than a fall from £3 million to £2.5 million over the five-year period would suggest.

The next phase, of the five years from 1960 to the end of 1964, saw profits before tax decline from £1.8 million to £1.6 million, with particularly disappointing results of only

£700,000 in both 1961 and 1962. Compared with the previous phase, these results were also worse than they appear, not only because of inflation affecting real values, but also because, unlike the earlier period, they now benefited from the contribution which the steel foundries made. In balance sheet terms there was also a deterioration. From £3 million net cash in 1960, net debt was £2.2 million in 1964, although this largely reflected the acquisition of the C. F. Taylor companies, the Pulsometer transaction, and the purchase of the minority shareholders in Peacock Brothers in Canada.

The third phase, covering the years from 1964 to 1972, saw profits before tax at a consistent level of around £2.4 million on average. Certainly there was no growth, but the balance sheet certainly changed. In 1965 a debenture issue of £2.5 million was made. However the acquisitions in 1969/70 of Harland Engineering and Osborn Hadfield and of a 50 per cent interest in Worthington Simpson led to a substantial increase in net debt, rising to £15 million in 1969, and to £23 million in the subsequent three years. This resulted in gearing of over 100 per cent in 1972. With hindsight – always so easy – it can be said that there were three main reasons for the stretched financial position in which the company now found itself.

The first of these was a number of strategic errors, some of which have already been touched on. The purchase of William Simons, added to the later acquisition of Lobnitz, was one obvious and serious error, in which the cost of the transactions was compounded by the heavy losses these businesses made. The heavy investment in Weir Housing was based on a misreading of the public housing market's likely acceptance of its design and manufacturing philosophy; this increased the operational gearing of the business at a time of lower demand and increasing competition, and its structure and management was not suited to entering the growing private housing market on a serious scale, which might have compensated. And the purchase of C. F. Taylor and entry into the aircraft equipment sector was something of a disappointment; it depended on the British civil aircraft industry performing much more strongly than in fact it did, and in order for it to have met expectations, a degree of official support would have been required that was not forthcoming. It was therefore basically an over-optimistic venture, which moreover was not strongly enough managed.

The second reason for the financial difficulties was a number of operational problems which produced poor results at several of the subsidiary companies. The Bahamas desalination contract was one example. The continuous poor results of Weir-Pacific was another, compounded by the heavy losses of a minor acquisition, of the instrumentation company Dobbie MacInnes. There were in addition some basically unrewarding initiatives such as Pacific Pumps and Clark Compressors. All of these were unsuccessful due to management failure of one sort or another. Of course, only idiots (and perhaps some investment analysts) expect managements to get everything right all the time, but there were undoubtedly too many misjudgements.

On the other hand there were some very positive achievements, both strategically and operationally. Weir Housing, for example, before its ill-conceived over-investment decision, produced very good returns in many years. A steel foundry division was built up from nothing, as much by excellent management and investment as by acquisition, into the best operation in the country. In pumps, a leading position was secured – albeit at considerable expense – on to which in time an excellent business could be built, as indeed was to happen. Whether the net balance was negative or not the reader must judge, and doubtless the verdict depends on whether a long or short term view is taken. In 1972, however, the position of the company was, as can be seen, not a very strong one in financial and particularly in balance sheet terms.

The third factor which led to this position, and which to a substantial degree explains many of the strategic and most of the operational failures, was something quite different and probably crucial. This was a clash of personalities, which during much of this period was a key influence. In every business there is always the dilemma (common also to government) of giving enough freedom to operators down the line, but at the same time keeping strong enough control from the very top to ensure overall success. Few ever really succeed in achieving the balance consistently, although many claim to do so, but all are aware of its necessity.

In Weir's, the situation was to become an unfortunate one. In 1954, at the start of the period, the two most senior executives below the chairman were J. R. Lang and Neil Niven. They each acted as chairman of a number of the subsidiary companies for which they had oversight and responsibility, although each subsidiary had its own managing director.

From 1968 a much more formal structure was put into place, with five operating divisions covering Engineering, Water, Housing, Aircraft Equipment and Foundries and Engineering Supplies. Engineering was the responsibility of J. W. Atwell (later Sir Jack Atwell); he had originally been recruited from Stewarts and Lloyds, the steel tube makers, as works manager at Cathcart. Water was managed by A. C. Smith, formerly sales director at Cathcart; Housing by Arthur Cargill; Aircraft Equipment by C. F. Taylor; and Foundries and Engineering Supplies by Steve Finch. All of these executives progressively became directors on the main board of the company. John Young was finance director, and for a period also company secretary. From 1968 I was planning director.

The problem was that there were considerable tensions between several of these individuals. J. R. Lang and Neil Niven did not get on with each other. Young held a poor opinion of Lang, but was a close friend of A. C. Smith. Steve Finch did not have much time for the others, apart from A. C. Smith and John Young. A. C. Smith, who had worked as sales director under J. R. Lang, had serious reservations about him, and also about J. W. Atwell. For my part, my sympathies were very much with A. C. Smith, John Young and Steve Finch.

The consequence of these poor personal relationships was bad communications, and also, particularly in the case of Neil Niven and J. R. Lang, a rivalry which affected business judgements. One side tended to push for emphasis and support being put behind the businesses in their patch, often regardless of the merits of other alternatives and, by definition, the best interests of the Group. The result was therefore, in order to avoid serious internal conflict on the board, often a compromise agreement to pursue the initiatives of all the parties concerned, when in reality the company could not afford to do so. One particular field of conflict arose over the pump activities of G. & J. Weir, championed by Lang and Atwell, and Drysdale's, championed by Niven.

The simple solution would have been to appoint an overall chief executive of the Group. In fact, prior to 1968, and the formal adoption of five operating divisions, this was exactly what Peter Lawson of PA Consultants had proposed. Lawson had suggested that Steve Finch should be the chief executive, which was logical, as he clearly appeared to be the best manager, but this solution was absolutely unacceptable to Niven, Lang and J. W. Atwell. (In Atwell's case, it is possible that he had hopes of himself being appointed chief executive. That would have been a mistake. Although hard working, diligent and loyal to the company he did not have the commercial and business outlook needed, and did not build good personal relationships very easily.) The opposition of three of the six senior executives, who were also main board directors, produced a serious crisis for the chairman. He chose to avoid the severe dislocation and public row and resignations which insistence on Finch's appointment would have caused. Instead the divisional structure already described was adopted. It should be noted that this compromise also resulted in J. J. B. Young leaving the Group in 1967, although he was later to return.

This leads inevitably to some consideration of the role of the chairman, Lord Weir – my father – in all this. He was someone of great charm, and was excellent in dealing with people, and thus greatly liked and respected. He had great integrity and an excellent knowledge of the business and of the industries in which it operated. He was a first class salesman, and indeed before becoming managing director after the war had been mainly involved on the sales side. He believed in consensus and in employing people whom he liked. He was also, like his own father before him, strongly international in his outlook and a great admirer of American business. In this he was much influenced by his early training in the USA with General Electric in their great turbine works at Schenectady (he had become a foreman in their experimental test facility), and by his membership of the board of International Nickel. He was also a more sophisticated businessman than his colleagues.

Again with the benefit of hindsight, he was probably

not tough enough when the crisis arose over the proposed appointment of Steve Finch as chief executive. Perhaps Steve Finch might have accepted the role of remaining in charge of the foundries – which were after all his great enthusiasm – if someone else had been brought in from outside as chief executive. Who knows? Certainly Finch as chief executive would have insisted on major changes in the senior personnel and in the management structure. However that is all speculation and the situation in 1972 was what it was, and in the next chapter we will see what then emerged.

Whatever might have been, however, the hard facts are that the Group found itself in a vulnerable financial position in 1972. Turning this around posed a real challenge – but one that had to be met if the Group was to survive, let alone flourish.

5

New regime
1972–9

As had been the case twenty years before, when an entire generation of senior management had retired, by early 1974 the key members of the board had all changed. Kenneth Weir had retired as chairman, as had J. R. Lang, the deputy chairman, and John Lord and Sir Charles Connell, the senior non-executive directors. J. W. Atwell, who had charge of the Engineering Division, retired in 1974.

I took over as chairman in 1972, and in 1974 S. L. Finch and J. J. B. Young became deputy chairman and managing director respectively. G. F. Arkless and Dr George Weir, a younger son of Kenneth Weir, joined the board in 1972 to strengthen its technical expertise, and Jean de Raemy joined in 1973 in order to give a greater emphasis to international business.

George Arkless had joined G. & J. Weir in the late 1950s from Hamworthy, a competitor in marine pumps. He had trained at C. A. Parsons and was an excellent and original designer who played a key part in developing new products, such as the ingenious water-lubricated turbo feed pump, and improving the existing range, particularly the key line of power station boiler feed pumps. Dr Weir was a brilliant academic mind. He had been a scholar at Cambridge where he took a double first in mechanical engineering and mathematics, and subsequently became an MSc in chemical engineering at Massachusetts Institute of Technology, followed by a PhD in physics. He was offered an excellent job with NASA in the American space programme, but declined on the somewhat unusual grounds that Houston 'had second class horse racing and no grouse shooting at all'. Quite how the recruiters in NASA's personnel department reacted to this is not known. He took over the planning function from me. Jean de Raemy was a Swiss engineer who had originally trained and worked with General Electric in the United States and subsequently for SGS, the well-known Swiss inspection and certification company.

The state of affairs in 1972 was not very encouraging. The Group was heavily indebted, with gearing of over 100 per cent as a result of the considerable cost of previous acquisitions and capital investment. This was compounded by the problems of some unfavourable major contracts, difficulties in the housing business and unfortunate ventures such as Simons-Lobnitz.

A further problem lay in the nature of one part of the debt, which consisted of 10-year 7.25 per cent deutschmark bearer notes. These had been issued for the acquisition of the 50 per cent holding in Worthington Simpson three years before, and initially they had appeared – to both Weir's and their partner in that transaction, Studebaker-Worthington – to be an attractive proposition. Unfortunately the rapidly rising strength of the deutschmark against sterling and the dollar meant that the amount of the liability in those currencies increased dramatically. The debt cost Weir's over £3.5 million in provisions until it was redeemed in

1975. Although then protected against further adverse exchange rate movements, the loan from Finance Corporation for Industry which replaced it carried a very high interest rate of 15.5 per cent on two thirds of it. Although Worthington Simpson performed very reasonably, its profits did not come anywhere near to covering the increased direct and indirect costs of this liability.

The Group's operating companies were experiencing mixed fortunes. The housing company, the aircraft division and the UK part of the hydraulic seals business were either making inadequate returns or actual losses. In desalination, Weir Westgarth had drastically reduced its staff and cut costs in the face of weak demand, but remained in a position to take advantage of any upturn in the desalination market. On the other hand Peacock Brothers in Canada was now operating satisfactorily. Moreover, acquisitions and a heavy investment programme had made the steel foundry operations the leaders in the UK, and in the persons of S. L. Finch and Alan Brearley they had much the best management in the industry.

In pumps too, the position was transformed from that of a few years earlier. The acquisition of Harland Engineering had made Weir Pumps the UK industry leader. The agreement with Studebaker-Worthington had given Weir's a 50 per cent interest in Worthington Simpson, a leading British standard pump manufacturer. As part of that agreement, Weir Pumps now had access to the US market through the formation of Worthington-Weir. This provided a jointly owned assembly plant in Maryland, with the sales outlet of the Worthington organisation.

There were two main challenges facing Weir Pumps, however. The first was for the company to integrate into one effective unit the three pump businesses which had previously been independently operated by G. & J. Weir,

Drysdale and Co., and Harland Engineering. The task was certainly challenging, but the potential benefits were great. In addressing the task, the Weir senior management under J. W. Atwell and subsequently J. R. Spence were reinforced by Kenneth Atchley and Ludwig Spiro from Harland, and, on the design side, by Harold Anderson, a highly talented engineer.

The second challenge was a strategic one, which was addressed at Group level. It was clear that the Harland acquisition had improved the international exposure of Weir Pumps to a limited degree, but mainly in Australia and South Africa. Worthington had given it at least the potential of US business. Nevertheless, the weighting of Weir's pump business was far too heavily concentrated in the UK. A particular weakness, given that the UK was shortly to join the EEC, was the lack of any significant involvement in continental Europe. Nor was there any local presence in either the Far East or South America. A series of initiatives to resolve this was therefore undertaken, mainly in cooperation with Worthington. It can fairly be said that from that time on, apart from a pause of a year or two caused by the problems which arose around 1980, an aggressive and expansionist policy was actively pursued for the pump business that has continued right up to the present day.

The first initiative was to try to acquire the German pump maker Halberg, which had its headquarters and a very large site in Ludwigshafen on the Rhine. Although Halberg had substantial assets it was operating poorly, and a modest price of £2.4 million was agreed with the owners. Financing in instalments was obtained locally, without recourse to Worthington or Weir. At the last minute, although Weir's and Worthington tendered payment as agreed, the owners of Halberg reneged in breach of contract and sold the company to a German competitor, SIHI. Surprisingly to those accustomed to the British and American legal systems, Weir's and Worthington were strongly advised that if they sued in the local courts where either the seller or SIHI were domiciled, as a foreign claimant there would be absolutely no possibility of them succeeding against a local company.

The Group was advised in Germany by the private bankers Schroder Munchmayer and Hengst. Their head was Ferdinand von Galen, a member of a noted noble family who had married the heiress to the Hengst bank, and whose uncle was the heroic Cardinal of Munich who had openly preached against the Nazis during the Second World War. They performed very well for the Group, but shortly afterwards ambition got the better of von Galen, who built up a major construction machinery group called IBH by dubious means and ended up in prison.

Next a similar attempt was made to purchase Pompes Guinard, the leading French pump maker. Dresser Industries of Dallas, the owners of Pacific Pumps, had previously attempted to buy Pompes Guinard and had been rebuffed on nationalistic grounds, so it was arranged for Weir and Worthington to buy it in partnership with the major French heavy engineer Creusot Loire. Again this effort came to nothing, due to the French insisting at the last minute that the pump interests of Jeumont Schneider be included.

Frustrated in these two endeavours, the possibility was examined of directly combining in some way the pump interests of Worthington outside the USA with those of Weir's. Worthington had been long established in Europe, with a significant presence in France and Spain, and was particularly strong in Italy, where it had an excellent and well-connected manager in Paolo Gamboni. During 1972 and 1973 a number of different possibilities were explored.

These ranged from a scheme along Royal Dutch/Shell lines to an outright sale to Weir's of the Worthington overseas businesses. This would have been well beyond Weir's own financial resources, but both the Prudential and Finance Corporation for Industry agreed to be financial partners in a new company which would comprise all of the Weir's and Worthington interests outside the USA. Much time and effort was expended on all these exercises, which were further complicated by taxation problems and also by changes in the senior personnel at Worthington. These personnel changes resulted in an inconsistent and changing attitude by Worthington towards the principle of the entire project. Eventually the process came to an end in 1974 with no result. Worthington's pump business was sold several years later to McGraw Edison of Chicago and was ultimately combined with the pump activities of Dresser and Ingersoll Rand.

The external business and economic background against which the Group had to operate from 1972 to 1979 was exceptionally unfavourable. Inflation was rampant, fuelled initially by irresponsible financial management, of which the most striking example was Tony Barber's expansionist budget in 1972. When Labour came to power in 1974, matters were not improved by the introduction of ill-thought-out interventionist policies. Industrial unrest was endemic and reached levels not seen for many years. There was a dramatic collapse in the stock market, triggered by the secondary bank crisis. Sterling was under pressure for much of the time. The very high rates of taxation in Britain, at one time reaching virtually 100 per cent on levels of income which would appear very modest today, represented a profound disincentive to effort or success. For much of the time the market for capital goods was poor, and international competition for the business available was intense, particularly from Germany and Japan. Altogether it was a bleak scenario, particularly for a company which started the period from a weak financial position, but needed somehow to address the dilemma of both improving its balance sheet and keeping up its momentum by investment, particularly in its steel foundry and pump businesses.

The Group did not have an easy year in 1972. There was a four-week strike at Cathcart and similar industrial problems at Worthington Simpson. There were also national strikes in the coal mining industry and the building trade, which seriously affected both the building division and the steel foundries. The foundries in particular suffered badly from interruptions in electricity supply, which disrupted their steel melting. In spite of all these difficulties, however, both the water and building divisions made modest profits, and overall the Group's profit before tax improved slightly to £2.55 million, despite being negatively affected by provisions against the deutschmark loan. A side effect of the industrial action was that a planned visit to Cathcart by the Duke of Edinburgh to mark the centenary of the company in that year had to be cancelled. As Buckingham Palace put it, 'His Royal Highness does not cross picket lines, you will understand.'

One bright spot was the first major North Sea pump order, obtained for BP's Forties field. On only one previous occasion had Weir's supplied pumps to the oil industry that were based on its own designs. This was in the 1930s, when Anglo-Iranian had installed at Abadan a cracker unit of major importance based on the then novel designs developed by Sun Oil. The system required hot oil pumps working at advanced conditions of pressure and temperature. The main contractor for the plant was the famous process engineering firm of M. W. Kellogg. Lord Weir and

Mr Kellogg had met when they were both crossing the Atlantic on the *Mauretania*, and they had formed a strong mutual admiration, as was not unlikely between two such distinguished engineers. As a result, Weir's was given the contract for this key equipment, without competition. The Weir's solution was to tackle the technical problem with what can only be described as brute force, involving units of massive proportions. It was a catastrophe. The pumps leaked the virtually explosive fluid they were handling and disaster was avoided only by the robust firewall which isolated them. Ironically they were replaced by an elegant design by Pacific Pumps, of which Weir's later became a licensee. Anglo-Iranian (managed, equally ironically, by Mr Ritchie and his successor of the Anglo-Persian pipeline fame) and Kellogg were to give no further orders to Weir's for many years.

The design for the Forties field was an innovative one, based on Weir's power station boiler feed pumps, and enabled the customer to renew the moving parts very rapidly, as they were made as a replaceable cartridge. Considerable help in winning this landmark order was provided by Mr Dancona of the Offshore Supplies Office and by the government's Scottish Office. It was the start of a long period of success worldwide, particularly for high-pressure water-injection pumps used for secondary recovery in oil fields.

The situation improved somewhat for the Group in 1973. Weir Pumps had numerous further successes in the North Sea, with orders from the Ekofisk, Forties, Brent, Piper and Auk fields. The order book for the Group improved sharply and was 40 per cent higher. Group profit before tax increased to £2.96 million, in spite of the building division making a heavy loss. This division suffered from an acute labour shortage, arising mainly because of

North Sea activity, and from a slowdown in private housing demand in the face of increased mortgage rates. Overall Group profits were substantially offset, however, by further heavy provisions due to the deutschmark rising strongly against sterling.

In the steel foundries a record market share was won, and teething troubles at the moulding line of the new Leeds foundry were gradually overcome. Apart from their precision casting business, profits were held back by the difficulty in recovering rapidly increasing costs. In the hydraulic seal business of Polypac, plans were put in hand for a new modern factory at Hartlepool, backed by a loan from the European Iron and Steel Community. In Italy their sister company, Polypac SpA, again produced excellent results and the Group increased its shareholding to 75 per cent. The aircraft equipment division had disappointing results but improved its workload with many new orders for aircraft galleys, particularly for British Airways' new fleet of Boeing 747s. (The cost of the design, manufacture and testing of the prototype galley for the 747 was over £1 million.) The Water division completed two major plants in Abu Dhabi in only thirteen months from order, and its Italian associate, SOWIT, won a large order in Libya.

The desalination operations of Weir Westgarth were combined with the condensing and power station heat exchanger business of Weir Pumps to form a single business, and in France a partnership arrangement was made with Delas, the heat exchange operation of the Alsthom company. The partnership quickly proved a great success, ultimately winning the condensing and feed heating orders for almost all of Electricité de France's massive programme of some fifty nuclear reactors. Another development during the year was the acquisition, in partnership with Lithgows – the former shipbuilders – of a 50 per cent interest in

Hasties of Greenock, the leading maker of ships' steering gear. This was considered to be a good fit with Weir's marine business. Hasties was then in the process of introducing a novel hydraulic pump, the key element in the steering system which had been designed by the National Engineering Laboratory in East Kilbride. In due course this was to prove a disastrous step.

During 1973, Frank Frame, who had been company secretary since 1968, became a director. He had joined the Group in fortuitous circumstances. He had been commercial manager of the UK Atomic Energy Authority, where he had been responsible for its nucleonics business, which subsequently became the highly successful company Amersham. Wishing to return to Scotland, he had written to Kenneth Weir asking whether he knew of any suitable opening. His letter arrived on the same day that Weir's newly appointed company secretary had said he could not move to Scotland after all, due to a family tragedy. Kenneth Weir then rang the Professor of Law at Glasgow University for a reference, and, on being told that Frame was one of the most brilliant students the professor had ever taught, immediately offered him the job. Subsequently Frame went to the Hong-Kong Shanghai Bank as legal adviser (being selected ahead of over twenty QCs) and rapidly rose to be the bank's vice chairman. He was also chairman of the *South China Morning Post*, which at one point had the distinction of being the most profitable newspaper in the world. He had a somewhat lugubrious expression – once very unkindly described as 'the face of an Irish famine' – that belied a wonderful dry sense of humour, allied to exceptional ability.

Profits before tax in 1974 were virtually unchanged at £3 million, but again the benefit was eroded by further gains in the deutschmark exchange rate and consequent heavy loan provisions. No progress was therefore made in

reducing the Group's gearing, and in fact it even increased
to the dangerous level of some 140 per cent. Up until that
time great efforts had been made, including senior management changes, to turn around Weir Construction. In 1974,
however, its losses were even worse, at £850,000. It was
therefore decided to sell it for whatever price the business
would fetch. Accordingly a 51 per cent stake was sold to
Ernest Ireland Ltd, with the balance to be acquired by them
over the following two years. Unfortunately, after eighteen
months Ireland got into severe difficulties. They could not
pay the balance and went into receivership. Fortunately, the
Group had retained the main part of the company's housing
land, which was worth over £1 million, and subsequently
disposed of it profitably and in stages.

A further disposal was the sale, to the Swedish company
ASEA, of Harland Simon, the electronics and control business which was part of the earlier acquisition of Harland
Engineering. Harland Simon specialised in the precision
control of drives for paper machines and steel mills. It was
a good enough business, and had supplied most of the
Canadian paper industry market, but had nothing in
common with the rest of the Group's activities. Improvement in the Group's gearing was not helped at this time by
worsening cash flow due to delays in output arising from
frequent late deliveries of key items such as castings and
electric motors.

At the operating level, Weir Pumps won a good level of
orders, but profitability on long-term contracts was
adversely affected by the inadequacies of the cost escalation
formula in coping with the nature and magnitude of infla-
tionary pressures. Elsewhere the situation was altogether
more cheerful. The desalination market turned up, with
orders for Saudi Arabia, Algeria, Qatar, Masirah and Abu
Dhabi. In France the first contracts for EdF nuclear plants

were won, and in Italy the SOWIT subsidiary won several good orders for power station heat exchangers, in partnership with the firm of Belleli. Rudolfo Belleli, the head of the firm, was a remarkable man. Of very diminutive stature, he had started out as a local plumber in Mantova after the war. He was the epitome of the northern Italian entrepreneur, and from modest beginnings had built up one of the very best steel fabrication businesses in Europe, with excellent facilities both in Mantova and in the south, next to the Finsider steel works at Taranto. From the latter he was able to fabricate and load out on board heavy-lift ships fabricated structures of over 1,000 tons. Not only did he manufacture all of SOWIT's power station heat exchangers, but he also supplied the fabrications for several of Weir Westgarth's desalination plants in the Middle East. Together with Belleli, SOWIT won thirteen consecutive power station heat exchanger orders, decimating the competition.

The steel foundries too had a better year in 1974, with the precision casting business again doing particularly well. The seal business did better in the UK, and Polypac SpA in Italy again performed very well. Aircraft equipment also improved its performance. Two new joint ventures were started up, both exploiting opportunities in the North Sea. Weir Houston was formed with Houston Engineers. Originally it marketed a curiously named product called the submersible bumper-sub, but it later went into the jar business. The jar is a hydraulic device which is used in an oil well when a drilling bit becomes stuck. It delivers, when activated, a massive blow in either an upward or downward direction to dislodge the bit. The jars were rented out to the oil companies who were also liable for the cost of reconditioning them when they were damaged, as often happened. Special jar manufacturing equipment was installed at Cathcart, and over the years it proved a very good venture.

The other development was Wood Weir, in partnership with the John Wood Group of Aberdeen. It undertook service work on machinery in the offshore oil industry, but it was something of a disappointment. There was doubtless a misunderstanding on Weir's part that as opportunities emerged to broaden the scope of North Sea activities these would come under the aegis of Wood Weir. It transpired that this was not the Wood Group's understanding, and they developed new activities themselves, aided at times by key staff they had recruited from Weir's. Wood went its own way and ultimately became the very successful business which it remains today.

In 1974, J. W. Atwell retired. He had originally joined the Group in 1961 from Stewarts and Lloyds as works manager at Cathcart, but soon rose to become the head of the Engineering Division, and therefore played a major part in the Group's affairs, particularly at Weir Pumps. He was primarily a production man, and prior to joining Weir's had not had much experience either in sales and marketing or on the technical side of the business. A most important contribution he made was to increase the recruitment of graduate engineers. He was very hard working, but, in all fairness to him, he did not really have the dynamism or commercial experience that was needed to drive Weir Pumps forward. Moreover, he did not always have good relations with his colleagues in the other operating divisions.

During the year another change to the board was the appointment of Lord Polwarth as a non-executive director. He was prominent in Scottish financial circles, and had been a government minister with North Sea oil responsibilities.

In 1975, profits improved markedly, almost doubling to £6.2 million. Turnover, reflecting the better order intake of the previous two years, exceeded £100 million for the first time. All the main operating companies performed satisfactorily. Weir Westgarth won a very large order in Qatar for four desalination plants, each producing 4 million gallons of fresh water a day. In France, the relationship between Delas and Weiritam was formalised with the creation of Delas Weir, in which the Group held a 45 per cent share. In truth the Group was entitled to a majority share, as Delas was nothing like as good a business as Weiritam, and EdF wanted Weiritam designs for their nuclear programme. French nationalism, however, prevailed, as EdF would not accept having a British controlled company as a major supplier. The compromise reached was that the new company had Weiritam's management and used its technology.

The most significant event of the year was the redemption of the deutschmark loan. A loan of £11.5 million was raised from Finance Corporation for Industry, and a rights issue of 1 share for 4 raised another £2.5 million. Almost £10 million of the proceeds was used to pay off the loan. This frightening figure represented the scale of appreciation in the German exchange rate against sterling in four and a half years. At the exchange rate when the loan was first taken out, its equivalent in sterling was just over £5 million. Clearly this had not been a very clever decision, and was a major adverse factor in the struggle to reduce the Group's gearing. Moreover the terms of the FCI loan were very severe.

In 1975, the first proposals for inflation accounting emerged with the publication of the Sandilands report. The report's somewhat theoretical approach involved considerable practical problems and generally it was not well received by industry. The comment in the Weir Group annual report read, 'If by the time Sandilands is understood and accepted we have not reduced inflation to a level which makes it unnecessary, we will be looking at our whole social and economic structure in an entirely new light.' This report was followed by the Morpeth proposals in the following year which drew the remarks: '… bias towards an academic and theoretical approach to accounting. There is little use making a laudable attempt to produce a more true and fair view if it merely leads to complexity and confusion.' Although these exercises were dropped in time, the temptation for the intellectuals of the accounting world to introduce change on a continuous basis sadly seems to remain as strong as ever.

Profits again improved in 1976, to £7.5 million before tax. Gearing improved too, with £20 million debt compared with £31 million in shareholders' funds. Although still too high, it was a vast improvement on the gearing of some 150 per cent seen two years previously. A major initiative to improve the efficiency of Weir Pumps was undertaken. It involved considerable investment in new machine tools, modernisation of the former Harland foundry at Alloa, and, most importantly, the decision to close the former Drysdale's plant at Yoker. The Yoker plant was not only on the opposite bank of the Clyde from Cathcart, but also some miles from it. In an attempt to avoid heavy redundancy costs, and indeed industrial action, it was decided to take the gamble of offering jobs at Cathcart to all at Yoker. In the event this decision proved correct, as few wanted to undertake the additional travel involved. Also during the year, Duncan MacLeod, a senior partner in the accountants Ernst and Whinney, joined the board as a non-executive director to strengthen its financial expertise.

Although it was a poor year for the foundry industry generally, the Group foundries increased their profit by 35 per cent. In desalination new orders were excellent. A consortium with Kraftwerk Union and Deutsche Babcock of

Germany won the Jeddah III contract, in which the water element was worth £40 million for four plants, each of 5 million gallons per day capacity. This was followed by an order from Dubai Aluminium for six plants of 4 million gallons per day output, while Sumitomo Heavy Industries, Weir Westgarth's licensee, was awarded a major contract for Dubai Electricity.

The execution of the Jeddah contract proved of interest. Some of the consortium employed Jamaican welders. They lived on a ship just outside territorial waters and could enjoy rum and other pleasures. A small difficulty was that they wanted to use the open area in the consortium's camp for cricket, whereas the Germans preferred football. Alcohol was, of course, strictly forbidden in Saudi Arabia. A precious supply of Johnny Walker was however kept in a large safe in the camp. If the religious police came, then the manager on duty, if he was German, was to say he could not open it as one of Weir's people had gone to Scotland with the key – and vice versa. On the same subject, a meeting with Weir's agent (who was also a furniture importer) had to be suddenly adjourned when he had an urgent message from one of his people at the docks to say that part of a shipment of sofas was leaking. Shipping was a real problem during the Saudi boom of those days, with long queues of ships waiting to unload. Hotel accommodation was very scarce, but fortunately Weir's agent owned a hotel himself. A classic scene was witnessed there when an elderly and very smartly dressed American banker went up to the Indian clerk at the desk and efficiently produced a letter with the words, 'I have a reservation.' After looking into his files for a while the clerk replied, 'Indeed, sir, you have a reservation, but I do not have a room.'

The main body of each desalination unit for Jeddah was built in one massive fabrication of hundreds of tons in the

Sumitomo plant in Japan. At Jeddah it was offloaded by the tackle of a heavy-lift ship on to a special trailer fitted with hydraulic jacks and sitting on a barge. On shore the trailer was dragged to the site. The plant was raised by the jacks and then lowered on to the foundations. In this ingenious way the problem of finding many highly expensive welders at site was avoided.

Other developments in 1976 included winning a major order from Aramco in Saudi Arabia for water injection pumps to pressurise oil wells, and a number of nuclear pumps for the Tennessee Valley Authority in the USA. The decision to increase investment in the Peacock Brothers facility in Montreal was reversed due to the political situation in Quebec and the rise of local nationalism, and the centre of operations was moved over the years to new facilities outside Toronto. Weir Group International was formed to oversee foreign operations. Its directors included Bill Vandersteel from New York, Denis Defforey, founder of the great Carrefour company, and Jack Williams, formerly head of Worthington's operations in Europe. The Weir Education Trust was also formed to help employees' children, and direct elections were put in place for the employee representatives on the trustees of the main pension fund.

Although the Group had made a fairly satisfactory profit overall in 1976, this was in spite of problems at the aircraft equipment companies, who had a poor year. The hydraulic seal business prospered as usual in Italy, but the move to a new factory in Hartlepool was disastrous, with poor management compounding the inevitable disruption caused by the transfer. Weir Construction (now 49 per cent owned) did show a profit, but Ernest Ireland, the majority shareholder, went bust. And among the associate companies, Hasties was put into receivership and sold to its competitor, Brown Brothers.

Sadly the year also saw the death of Kenneth Weir, the retired chairman. Apart from everything he did for Weir's, and his sterling service in artillery production in the war, he was also a director of Dunlop, International Nickel and the Royal Bank of Scotland.

The next year, 1977, showed a further improvement in profits to £9.1 million. The aircraft equipment division was sold to the EIS company. Investment continued in Weir Pumps with a new research and development laboratory at Alloa and the establishment of product manufacturing centres there and at Cathcart. Service centres were set up in Qatar and Abu Dhabi. The steel foundries had a difficult year, but made good progress developing overseas markets, particularly in the United States. The seal companies continued the pattern of poor results in the UK and an excellent performance in Italy. In desalination, no major contracts were booked, but orders for two small plants were won in the remote north of Saudi Arabia, at Al Wajh and Duba, certainly the most difficult environment in which the Group ever had to work. There was no road access, and a small harbour had to be built first to bring in the equipment. Gearing remained at some 60 per cent. In spite of the generally difficult conditions, an improvement in profits was forecast for the next year.

That promise was not fulfilled in 1978, though, and profits dropped back to £7.6 million. The balance sheet improved, showing debt of £17 million and shareholders' funds of £48 million, but this result was somewhat cosmetic, reflecting as it did a substantial revaluation of land and buildings. Weir Pumps and the steel foundries shared very disappointing results due to serious strikes at both Cathcart and Leeds, and more working days were lost in 1978 than in the previous ten years combined. The foundry market was very difficult, and overseas work began to be affected by the exchange rate. John Ferguson joined the foundries from British Leyland as managing director. The seal business at Hartlepool again showed substantial losses. Lucien Wigdor joined the board in a semi-executive capacity as chairman of Weir Pumps, with the object of keeping a tighter oversight and control over its operations.

There were bright spots, however. Desalination showed a profit of £3.4 million, quite apart from the profit Weir Pumps made on supplying equipment to them. Delas Weir obtained very good orders in France. Weir Pumps obtained major contracts for Drax power station in the Midlands and for nuclear pumps for the Tennessee Valley Authority, together with much business in the water supply industry. A new seal factory was opened in Livorno, and as chairman I made a speech on Tuscany TV in fluent Italian (I memorised it, as I did not speak a word of the language). It was the only new factory built in the area that year, and the local archbishop, the prefect and the Communist mayor, who all detested each other, attended the opening in the hope of each getting credit for it. The workforce, who were mainly female, celebrated with a dance in the canteen at lunchtime.

On a more dignified note, Her Majesty The Queen opened the desalination plant for Dubai Aluminium during her tour of the Middle East, which some locals described as the most important visit since that of the Queen of Sheba. She was presented, as was Sheikh Raschid, the Ruler, with a gold cup enamelled, appropriately for a Scottish company, with a thistle motif, and today it is the centrepiece of the dining table at Holyrood.

In spite of the difficulties experienced during the year, there was optimism about prospects for 1979. As previously remarked, the two challenges, which were clearly difficult to meet simultaneously, were to improve gearing and to maintain – by investment or other steps – the momentum in growth and better efficiency.

Certainly gearing had improved from 100 per cent in 1972 (and even higher in some years) to a more comfortable level of around half that. Over the period, expenditure on fixed assets (taking no account of government grants) was £24.3 million compared with total depreciation of £11.2 million. There was no question therefore about the Group's willingness to invest. The bulk of the expenditure had been at Weir Pumps and the steel foundries. In the former it showed in more modern machine tools, a new research and development facility, a modernised foundry, product centres and better information technology. In the foundries the consistently profitable precision casting company at Holbrook had been much expanded. Elsewhere melting facilities, non-destructive testing capability, and new fettling and heat treatment facilities had been put in to make the steel foundries not only the largest but also certainly the best equipped in the UK. New hydraulic seal production factories had also been built in Hartlepool and Livorno.

As for those businesses which had been performing poorly in 1972, aircraft equipment and housing had been sold, although it can certainly be argued that too much time was spent (with accompanying losses) in fruitlessly trying to turn around the latter. In desalination, Weir Westgarth had developed from simply ticking over on a small scale to emerge finally as a substantial business with good profits. In power station heat exchange, Delas Weir in the French nuclear programme and SOWIT in Italy had been exceptional successes. Measured in terms of turnover, the Group had advanced from £65 million in 1972 to £183 million by 1978, although the increase in real terms was obviously considerably less as a result of inflation during the period. In the final years of the period a substantial volume was however represented by desalination plant and power station heat exchange, where much of the manufacture was largely subcontracted.

Nevertheless the period had undoubtedly shown progress. Unfortunately any gains were to be shortlived. A serious setback was just around the corner.

6

Disaster and recovery
1979–83

A very dramatic period in the Group's history began in
1979. The first few months of the year were quiet enough,
and showed little evidence of what was to come. Indeed in
March, although reporting pretax profits for 1978 somewhat lower at £7.6 million – mainly as a result of unofficial
strikes – considerable optimism was expressed. In the report
for 1978, I had said, 'We expect to see a sharp recovery in
earnings in 1979, with a resumption of the growth which
was interrupted last year.' Such was the confidence, indeed,
that the board proposed to increase the final dividend.

At the same time several expansive initiatives were
pursued. These included a substantial investment in Mexico
in the new Acerlan steel foundry, part of the Lanzagorta
company, which was mainly a valve manufacturer supplying most of the requirements of Pemex, the state oil
monopoly. This business owed much to the personal relationship, of a typically Latin American kind, between Señor
Lanzagorta – a Spanish emigrant from the Basque country
– with the top management of Pemex. Other opportunities
being pursued were to enter the precision investment

castings business. Although the foundry at Holbrook outside
Sheffield, originally acquired from Samuel Osborn, had
been considerably expanded and had been consistently
successful, its precision casting business was confined to
high quality shell moulding, and it was not involved in lost-
wax investment casting, perhaps the only high margin and
high growth sector of the industry. Accordingly the
company engaged in negotiations with two leading firms,
the L. E. Jones company in Minnesota, and P. I. Castings of
Altrincham in Cheshire. At the same time it was hoped to
improve the outlook for Weir-Pacific Valves by the acquisition of Cannon Valve, who had a complementary and
apparently successful line in larger ball valves.

By the middle of the year, prospects had deteriorated
sharply and suddenly owing to a combination of events
which continued unabated for the next eighteen months
and quickly led, as will be seen, to a major financial crisis.
Some of these events were beyond the control of the
company, but others were not, or at least should have been
either foreseen or more quickly countered. Even with
hindsight, however, it is difficult to say whether the end
result would have been very different if remedial action had
been taken more rapidly. The external problems of industrial unrest, poor demand and the adverse effect of the
exchange rate on exporters were not confined to the Weir
Group, but caused great difficulty to many other manufacturers, particularly in the engineering industry. Taken
together, these events produced a very formidable series of
challenges.

In the Group's steel foundries, the early part of 1979 saw
the continuation of a strike at Catton's, the largest of the
operations. Soon afterwards the market turned down badly
for all the foundries with a deterioration in both demand
and prices. This was compounded as the year went on by

the strengthening in sterling as a result of both necessary monetary tightening by the government and the strong increase in North Sea oil production, with the resulting reaction of international capital markets. (At the time, George Soros, the well-known international investor, remarked to me of government policy, 'The cure is right, but I hope it does not kill the patient.') For the foundries the exchange rate effect was serious as they had laudably and successfully increased their export business in the previous year or two, particularly in the USA. There they had won considerable orders from such top class customers as Caterpillar. The difficulty of that particular achievement should not be underestimated, as Caterpillar was perhaps the most demanding of all customers. Unfortunately the foundries had also gained substantial orders from a couple of American valve companies and from IBH in Germany (the business developed in construction machinery by Graf von Galen) and these all failed, eventually leaving the foundries with significant bad debts.

As the year ground on, matters went from bad to worse for the steel foundries. In some months, orders as a whole hardly reached 50 per cent of national industry capacity. Moreover Weir's investment in Acerlan in Mexico turned out badly. The local management would not accept Weir's proposals for operating the business, where in any event demand had turned down. Unfortunately, like many businesses in Mexico, it had been financed with borrowings in US dollars. When the Mexican peso collapsed there was an immediate and severe financial problem. Initially Weir's put up more capital, but when they rightly refused to do more their investment was diluted and eventually had to be written off. Certainly there was a lesson to be learned from dealing with Latin American partners, who seemed to have an extraordinary ability for personal survival at the expense of others. At home, the Group businesses worst hit by the difficulties in the steel casting industry were Alston Foundry and Osborn Hadfield Steel Founders in Sheffield. By the end of 1979 it had become clear that they had to be closed.

Alston was located in a remote part of Cumberland, in the town of Alston, which claims to be the highest market town in England. (Buxton in Derbyshire also makes the same claim, pointing out that Alston lacks a *regular* market.) It had been purchased from the Steel Group, whose excavator business was a very important customer, and who virtually made its acquisition by Weir's a condition of their continuing business. Alston's inaccessibility could hardly be overstated. Shortly after the foundry was bought, it was decided to hold a Group board meeting there in the middle of May. The town's remoteness and altitude were conclusively demonstrated by the fact that the meeting had to be abandoned due to snow. Alston did however produce a most unusual event. One day the manager rang me, as the Group chairman. First he asked whether I was alone, as he had a very confidential matter to disclose. On being assured this was the case, he then made the astounding statement, 'We have struck oil.' Apparently the small stream which divided the two parts of the factory – called the Nent Force – had quantities of oil bubbling up in it. Alas, this discovery did not transform the fortunes of the Group at a difficult moment. It transpired that there was an old pipe linking an oil tank on one side of the stream with the works boiler on the other side and it had corroded.

When the closure of Alston was announced early in 1980, the local MP was informed in advance, as was normal practice for such events. He was Willie Whitelaw, at that time Home Secretary. I knew him well, having first played golf with him at the age of sixteen before Willie had become a Member of Parliament. With typical courtesy, Willie insisted on meeting at a date and time convenient to me rather than to himself. He appeared with some members of the county council, and immediately showed how well informed he was by saying he was not surprised at all by the closure and knew it was due not only to poor trade but also to the bad industrial relations largely caused by a particular shop steward. All he wanted to do was ensure as much employment as possible for those laid off. He charmed the Group into letting the council have some of the buildings for new small businesses, and the scheme had some considerable success, including such unlikely activities as guitar making.

Osborn Hadfield was a different matter. Far more people were involved than at Alston. Some activity at the site was preserved, and a company, O. H. Hitech, was formed to take over the highly advanced non-destructive test facility. This was the highest powered X-ray facility in the UK. Indeed the protective door of the radiographic chamber weighed 120 tons. Its original purpose was to inspect heavy castings for nuclear reactor service (ironic, as Sheffield Council had declared the city 'A nuclear-free zone'), but it was also used even to observe RB211 jet engines internally for Rolls Royce while they were running. It also had excellent facilities for upgrading nuclear castings to the extremely high standards required. Necessary as these two closures were for the continuing viability of the Group's steel foundry operations, the decision brought very heavy costs in the shape of redundancy payments and write-offs.

On the engineering side matters were little better. From the middle of 1979 to the latter part of 1980 it became clear that there were serious problems at Weir Pumps. In part the market, particularly for exports, was not very helpful. The main difficulties, however, were internal ones. Management was not tight enough and it became clear that financial control was seriously deficient. Labour problems and strikes and a lack of commitment to improvement in efficiency by workforce and management compounded the problem. With time, it also became clear that pricing policy had gone badly wrong, and that many contracts had been optimistically accepted on the assumption of cost improvements, which subsequently and in reality were not realised. The continuing deterioration in Weir Pumps' performance resulted in the decision in mid 1980 to proceed with making up to 1,000 people redundant.

At Weir-Pacific Valves the struggle over several years to turn the business around, and in the course of which several senior management changes had been made, was finally abandoned, and by May 1980 their plant was closed and the residue of the business sold. Obviously this decision, and more importantly the redundancy programme at Weir Pumps, were to have very heavy financial costs in the short term.

In desalination, the successes by Weir Westgarth in the late 1970s produced much improved profits. By 1980, however, failure to win new orders had led to a significant redundancy of some 120 jobs. Again this gave rise to considerable cash costs. One problem Weir Westgarth increasingly faced was difficulty in obtaining bonds from the banks. Two main types of bonds were needed for the major contracts in the Middle East. The first was bid bonds, which were basically an assurance that the bidder would proceed with the contract if his bid was successful. The second was performance bonds, which were a guarantee that the bidder would perform in the terms of the contract. As the major contracts were at times worth £50 million or more, these were a substantial commitment by the banks who provided them, and their willingness to do so was obviously much influenced by their assessment of the financial state of the companies involved. Moreover the bonds were normally of the kind called 'on demand', which meant that the customer had the absolute right to call them at his own decision. In fact no 'on demand' bond had ever been arbitrarily called by a Middle East customer, but this understandably did not always reassure the banks, certainly in the UK.

The situation of Weir Westgarth's competitors was rather different. For example, on a major contract for Al Khobar in Saudi Arabia, Weir Westgarth formed part of a French consortium, the other members being Alsthom, the leading French civil contractor Boygues, and Technip, the French project engineer. The difference between French and UK government policy was stark. For a start, Weir's were told to consider themselves 'honorary Frenchmen'. They were told that winning the contract was considered by France to be a matter of national interest. Both bonding (at almost half the rate charged in the UK) and cash flow financing would be provided for Weir's and they were given full access to the French ambassador in Riyadh. Alas, although the Weir, Alsthom and Technip parts of the bid were lower than any competitors (and in Weir's case at a good profitable level), the Boygues price was quite out of line. By some clever negotiations with the customer, it was agreed that the consortium could substitute another civil contractor for Boygues, although this was distinctly irregular. In the end, M. François Boygues, their chairman, was offered $10 million in cash on signature of the contract if he agreed to let his part of the bid be subcontracted to others, and to be involved in name only. With stupendous Gallic arrogance, he said that 'the orange colours of Boygues will never be used as an umbrella for others'. In truth he was confident of getting a major hospital contract and could not carry out two very big jobs in Saudi Arabia at the same time. In any event this and some bad luck in other bids in Saudi Arabia meant that Weir Westgarth did not gain any major desalination contracts. One result of this was that there were no large down payments from such contracts, and these had contributed significantly in the recent past to the Group's cash flow. The other consequences were a costly redundancy at Weir Westgarth and the lack of an ongoing profit contribution from it.

The Group therefore was severely afflicted by a simultaneous combination of poor trading results, heavy costs of redundancy payments and plant closure, and rapidly rising debt. When we look at the overall position, therefore, and consider the financial effects during 1979 and 1980, it makes for grim reading. At the start of 1979 the balance sheet showed loan capital and bank loans of £29 million offset by £12 million in cash and short term deposits. At the end of the year, debt had increased to £47 million, offset by only £6 million in cash. In twelve months, therefore, there had been an adverse swing of no less than £24 million. A further but less significant deterioration was apparent in 1980. There were other consequences, too. During 1979 and 1980, shareholders' funds had fallen from £48 million to £26 million, and gearing had increased to some 170 per cent. Moreover, net current assets, which had been £20 million at the start of 1979, were by the end of 1980 minus £1 million. Interest charges, which were £2.5 million in 1978, increased dramatically to £4.5 million and £7.4 million in the two following years.

As the financial position began to deteriorate from the spring of 1979 onwards, discussions and negotiations began, first with FCI, the major provider of loan capital to the Group, and later with the Royal Bank of Scotland, who were, with Lloyds and Williams and Glyn's, the main source of unsecured overdraft finance. In March 1979, FCI agreed to changes in the terms of their loans, thus providing some breathing space. In September the Royal Bank agreed to increase their facility from £7 million to £11 million, but this was soon seen to be insufficient to meet the Group's rapidly escalating needs. Accordingly, from then onwards and throughout 1980, recourse was had on a piecemeal basis to several other banks and also to discounting of bills. These new lenders included Toronto Dominion Bank, Grindlays, Bank of Montreal, Algemeine Bank Nederland, and, for the largest amount of these increased facilities, Bank of America and the HongKong Shanghai Bank. Most of these facilities were quite short term. The number of lenders was in itself to prove a real problem when further negotiations were eventually needed, and although the Royal Bank was leader of the lending group it was not always easy to get the unanimity required for important decisions. Indeed, at one moment when a disagreement arose, Michael Sandberg, the chairman of the HongKong Shanghai Bank, was even interrupted at Lord's while watching a test match. He was not happy. The position was further complicated by the fact that several of these banks not only did not undertake bonding business but were not even familiar with it, and bonding was to become a serious problem.

By early 1980 it appeared that unless a major disposal could be made at a decent price, the Group was likely to exceed its borrowing capacity. No such disposal was in sight. The final dividend was omitted, and in July another round of discussions started with the banks and FCI. The former were now seriously concerned at the level of unsecured borrowings. Their support was necessary to ensure that the interim results for the first half of 1980 could be prepared on the basis that the company was still a going concern. Agreement was reached to continue to support the Group provided that a range of floating and fixed charges over the main subsidiaries was given, and that an independent report on the financial situation was prepared by Peat, Marwick, Mitchell, the leading accountants.

At the same time the board, recognising the lack of confidence which they and the banks had developed in him, dismissed Eric Bremner, the finance director. In his place Ian Boyd was appointed as finance controller. In that capacity, and soon after as finance director, he served with great competence and distinction for many years. At the main subsidiary, Weir Pumps, which had been at the heart of the operating problems, Ramsay Spence was replaced by his deputy, Ron Garrick. After 1981 Garrick became chief executive, and, as will be seen, he later led the Group first to recovery and then to great success.

The insistence by the banks and FCI for holding fixed and floating charges then led to a considerable complication, as it appeared this would breach the terms not only of the quoted unsecured loan stocks but also of the Group's two debentures. Lengthy negotiations ensued, and these delayed addressing the real financial problem. In the end the loan stocks were repaid and any problem with the debentures was neutralised, first by an 'Instrument of Alteration' and then by redemption.

By Christmas 1980, the report by Peats was delivered. It was reasonably favourable, but pointed out, not surprisingly, deficiencies in Weir Pumps' financial control, although by then the new management had moved well forward in addressing these. By this time, however, Rea Brothers, who had been the Group's financial advisers for some ten years, had been joined by Hill Samuel under Sir Robert Clark. A close watch on events had been maintained by the Bank of England through Lord Benson, its senior adviser. He told me that the clearing banks did not consider Rea Brothers of sufficient weight and that the Group had to bring in someone else in addition. I, who had myself been a director of the Bank of England for several years, chose Sir Robert, who was a colleague of mine. In truth Sir Walter Salomon at Rea Brothers had not exactly endeared himself to the clearing banks by his attitude towards all of them. In his view they were not real bankers like himself but were 'functionaries'. His feelings were reciprocated by them.

When the Peat report was discussed with Finance for Industry, or FFI (as FCI were now styled), and the banks in January, to the considerable surprise of John Young who was representing Weir's, new demands were made. By then the banks were coming to the conclusion that a support operation of the sort required was only likely to be acceptable to them if new money were also injected either from a sale of assets or from an issue of some kind. Their proposals therefore included disposal of a major subsidiary, although how that could be achieved at any sort of price in the business conditions then prevailing was rather difficult to understand. They also required Professor Rorke of Heriot Watt University to report on the viability of Weir Pumps. Again. quite how an academic, even of good technical ability, could really do this was not easy to see, and basically it was not very fair to have asked him. In February 1981, Rorke reported and confirmed that Weir Pumps had many strengths, although he rightly pointed out problems in production costs. As with the earlier criticisms by Peats, however, these were already being actively addressed, not only by the major redundancy that had been made, but also by the energetic and effective actions Ron Garrick was now undertaking.

After Rorke's report had been submitted to the banks, Sir Robert Clark presented to the board the conclusions of Hill Samuel and Rea Brothers. In summary these were: the share capital and reserves, which had been badly depleted, were insufficient; during the second half of 1981 it was likely that borrowing would exceed the agreed facilities; energetic asset disposal should be pursued, but Weir Pumps should remain the core of the business; no new bonds were to be obtained in the meantime; and £10 million of debt and interest should be converted into preference shares. Fortunately Sir Walter Salomon made a crucial suggestion, subsequently adopted, that an underwritten offer to share-holders of convertible preference shares should be made. At the time, however, it was far from clear how practical this was, and who would be prepared to be underwriters.

Incidentally, convertible preference shares may be common enough nowadays, but the first time they had previously been seen was when Weir's had bid some ten years earlier for Worthington Simpson. They were an origi-nal suggestion, if not outright invention, by Dr George Weir: subsequently it was found out that a small issue had been made in 1932 by a minor timber company on a Northern stock exchange. It was not a bad thought from a PhD in physics from MIT. (It should also be noted that one significant disposal was in fact made in 1981. That was the sale to the Dowty Group of the overseas Polypac business, principally Polypac SpA in Italy, and the closure of the Hartlepool factory in the UK. How ironic it is to recall that George Dowty had offered control of his whole company to Weir's in 1938 for a very modest sum.)

The board accepted the draft proposals, but when in March the formal offer was made there were a number of changes which they did not like. There were some condi-tions which would make it more difficult for the company to operate if the proposed capital reconstruction was suc-cessful and it returned to normality. For example, one con-dition was that the straight preference shares issued could only be redeemed by an issue of equity. (When the Group did eventually recover, it could be argued that this led to an unnecessary dilution of its share capital.) The restriction on raising new bid bonds or performance bonds was to become a particular difficulty for Weir Westgarth's and Weir Pumps' operations.

The most important feature of the proposals was that a rights issue of 10 per cent convertible preference shares would be made on the basis of one of these for one existing ordinary share, and at a price of 25p per share. The FFI Group and the Scottish Development Agency agreed to underwrite the issue. At that time FFI was jointly owned by the Bank of England and the clearing banks, and their decision to participate was very much influenced by Henry Benson, as chief adviser to the Governor. Equally the Scottish Development Agency took their decision with the support of the Scottish Economic Planning Department and of George Younger, the Secretary of State for Scotland at the time.

Sir Robert Clark then summoned the directors, excluding myself, to a meeting and said that it had been decided that I must go as a price for the lenders' support. The board protested strongly, but were eventually forced to agree. The following day, Sir Robert told me of the decision. Quite obviously the lenders had decided on this course of action some time previously, and indeed Clark admitted that the Royal Bank had originally proposed a quite different replacement chairman from Sir Francis Tombs, who was the final choice. I could hardly demur. Not only did the banks hold all the cards, but a few years before I had actually offered Tombs the job of chief executive, and I knew him well and respected him.

Nevertheless, the manner in which my dismissal was handled seemed to me to have been very underhand, and clearly implied that the banks thought I could not be trusted and dealt with in a frank and open way. Nor was there any recognition of the fact that my priority was that a great firm that my family had built up over generations should survive. Surely anyone would understand that if the price of survival was giving up my own position, then that was the reality which I would certainly face and accept. I had also concluded from all this that the lenders could not be trusted to have any commitment to the long term independence of the Weir Group, and I decided to act independently.

When Francis Tombs was appointed as chairman, the banks had initially wanted me to leave completely. Hector Laing, a fellow director of the Bank of England and a close friend of mine, had however told the Royal Bank – of which he was one of the largest customers – that this was totally unacceptable, and as a result I had become vice chairman.

I now contacted Derald Ruttenberg of Studebaker-Worthington. Ruttenberg had of course not only been a business partner with Weir's for some ten years, but we had also become close friends. Moreover he had a good understanding of the business, knew and liked the people in it, and had been kept well aware of the problems. He sent over one of his people and convinced himself that the steps which had been taken in 1980 gave a good chance of recovery. He then brought in Jacob Rothschild, who had not long before left N. M. Rothschild after disagreements with others in his family and had set up the firm of RIT.

Now when an underwritten rights offer is made to shareholders, as was the case with the proposed convertible preference issue, the practice is that on the closing date the brokers first offer in the open market those rights which the shareholders have not taken up. If they are not bought, these rights are passed on to the underwriters who then subscribe for them. Accordingly Ruttenberg and Jacob Rothschild bought these rights for about 1p per share, subscribed for them and thus ended up with some 80 per cent of the issue, and in effect – as the rights were one convertible preference share for one ordinary share – with the equivalent of 40 per cent of the Weir Group's equity.

The news of this coup was not well received. After all, virtual control of the company had passed overnight into the hands of friends of the just dismissed chairman. Francis Tombs sent for me and asked whether I had known about what was to happen and why had he not been told. I replied that I had indeed known, but that I had to respect confidentiality about the intended transaction, which in any event was in no way either irregular or improper. A little bit of spice was added by the fact that Francis Tombs was a director of N. M. Rothschild. Given the Bank of England's involvement with the lenders through Henry Benson, I was also sent for by the Governor and asked to explain myself. I replied that I saw nothing wrong in a large part of the Group's shares being in friendly and supportive hands. Doubtless it was a little naïve to have expected me to have told anyone in advance, given the distinct possibility that an attempt might very well have then been made to frustrate the whole operation.

Of course, if all this had not happened, a very large shareholding would have ended up in the hands of FFI and the Scottish Development Agency. Very possibly – and there was subsequently some evidence of this – control of the Group would eventually have been passed into other hands, perhaps to the Glasgow based Howden Group. Francis Tombs responded with very good grace and shortly afterwards invited Ruttenberg to join the board. Not only was that the right thing to do, but from a practical point of view it would hardly have been very sensible to have had major shareholders in the shape of two such formidable and activist people as Ruttenberg and Jacob Rothschild on the outside of the tent. Many years later in 2008, there was, for some of us who had been involved with the problems at Weir's at this time, perhaps a certain irony in the fact that the Royal Bank of Scotland itself needed to call for a gigantic rights issue and put two profitable subsidiaries up for sale in order to deal with difficult circumstances.

The events of 1981 were therefore very dramatic, and very wearing for those involved. The steps taken in 1980 and 1979 by way of closures, redundancies, reorganisation and management changes, combined with the capital reconstruction, had their effect. Whereas 1980 had shown the horrible result of £8.25 million loss before tax and almost £10 million loss after tax, 1981 showed a profit before tax of £8.3 million. The financial restructuring naturally had a beneficial effect on the interest charge, which dropped from £7.3 million to £4.7 million. Leaving interest out of the calculation, however, the profit before interest and tax in 1981 was £13 million, compared with a loss of almost £1 million in the previous year. Clearly the banks, however much they were justified in protecting their interests, had never believed that such a recovery would take place. That certainly showed in their attitude, and indeed, now that recovery had been demonstrated, one problem for the Group was the restrictions the lenders' conditions had placed on it. As a footnote of some cynical interest, when the 1981 results came out, the Lex column in the *Financial Times* wondered whether the dramas of the previous year had been totally justified.

Success of course, as the saying goes, had many fathers, and failures few if any, so perhaps it is worth some analysis of how the company, from a reasonably good performance from 1972 to 1978 in spite of the very difficult business background, managed to get into so parlous a position in 1979 and 1980, and indeed of why the disastrous downturn in its fortunes had not been anticipated sooner. Moreover, the optimistic tone expressed by the board in the spring of 1979 showed that subsequent events clearly came as a surprise. The actions taken in those two years, backed up by the financial restructuring, certainly restored the position, but this begs the question of whether the traumas could have been foreseen, and indeed if there were any actions which could have been taken sooner to have at least lessened the damage.

There were clearly a number of different reasons for the crisis, and it is a matter of opinion what weight should be attached to each. External circumstances, as have already been described, were very unfavourable from 1979 onwards, and indeed a number of other large companies, such as Stone Platt, encountered similar difficulties, and some of them did not recover. There were, however, clearly failures both in strategy and in day-to-day management. With hindsight it is easy enough to say that the emphasis put on expanding the scope of the steel foundry business, and investing so heavily in it, may have been a dubious strategy. The management of the foundries was first class, and by 1979 the facilities, when most of the investment programme had been carried out, were, like the management, the best in the industry. In several years good profits were indeed made, particularly at Catton's and on the precision casting side at Holbrook. The profit potential was never fully realised, however, not only because of too frequent industrial action, but also, and much more importantly, because of the cyclical nature of the foundry industry, a continuing decline in the fortunes and activity level of much of its customer base in the UK engineering industry, and overcapacity and the reluctance of inefficient and poorly equipped competitors to close their operations down even in the face of heavy losses. It was as if to say, by way of analogy, that a Rolls Royce is a splendid vehicle, but does not do so well on rough mountain tracks.

Further strategic problems had their roots in decisions taken a considerable time earlier, and some of these have already been touched on. Housing had no connection with the other parts of the company and, again with hindsight, should probably have been disposed of much sooner, while it was still making money. The aircraft equipment business never paid its way, and its acquisition was also a strategic error. The hydraulic seal business of Polypac was not a strategically mistaken acquisition; the great success of the Italian arm showed how profitable an exercise it could be. The problem lay with the UK operation, and the decision to invest so heavily in the new plant at Hartlepool, when the management of the operation was inadequate, certainly was wrong.

Turning then to the management of the Group during the period leading up to the crisis in 1979, several matters are clear. At the operating company level the management of Weir Pumps was crucial to the Group as a whole. In the event it was nothing like strong enough, particularly when circumstances became adverse. Moreover, although industrial relations were turbulent enough for the British engineering industry generally, Weir Pumps suffered considerably more than most. Whether their workforce was inherently more difficult, or whether management handled the issues worse than they should, is a matter of debate. What is not in doubt is that Weir Pumps' financial control was inadequate. Among other companies in the Group, not only were there the strategic mistakes in being involved at all – or for so long – in housing and aircraft equipment, but the management of both was inadequate. It would equally be unfair not to comment that management at other parts of the Group performed well, and, in cases such as Weiritam in France, Polypac in Italy and Peacock Brothers in Canada, acquitted themselves extremely well.

Finally, there is the question of the performance of the top management of the Group, where responsibility ultimately rested. For a start, financial control from the centre was not good enough, either in systems or in personnel. As a result a really strong ethos of financial discipline was not firmly rooted, and operating budgets were not respected in the way they should have been. Longer term forecasts, as in the Group's five-year plan, were consistently optimistic. Most importantly, however, the fundamental structure at the very top was wrong. Instead of having the structure, now almost universally accepted, of a separate chairman and strong chief executive, there was a loose arrangement of a nominally full-time chairman, in the shape of myself, and John Young as managing director. When the Group was hit by the problems already described, the managing director was almost continually engaged in firefighting at individual operating companies which were in trouble, and this was at the expense of exercising overall control. He worked tirelessly, but it was too much for anyone. As for myself as chairman (and here it is almost impossible to be objective, and rather akin to writing your own obituary), three comments are not unfair. First, I had too many distracting outside activities. I was a director of the Bank of England, of the major cable and construction group BICC, and of the British Bank of the Middle East; I was chairman of The Great Northern Investment Trust; and I was a member of the Engineering Industries Council and The Scottish Council, among other activities. In today's world of corporate governance, such wide involvement would not be well regarded. Second, I was insufficiently tough, both by temperament and in practice, with people and their performance. Certainly there were personnel changes that I either should have made or should have made sooner. Third, I was consistently too optimistic both about the likely outcome of actions which were taken and also about the potential danger of problems. Doubtless others may quite fairly add other items to the list. What can however be said positively is that the actions taken by the top management in 1980 led to a strong recovery in the following year, and that the Group did have the core strengths on which later success could be built.

The events leading up to the financial restructuring and the subsequent appointment of Francis Tombs as chairman led to substantial changes in the board. In 1980, C. F. Taylor, who was the founder of the aircraft equipment companies, retired. In 1981, Lucien Wigdor, who had been chairman of Weir Pumps, retired, as did S. L. Finch, who was deputy chairman of the Group as well as keeping a close watch on the foundry activities. He was unquestionably the doyen of the steel foundry industry and had led the Group's development in the premier position in the field. Ian Boyd became Group finance director, having been appointed finance controller the year before. Ron Garrick joined the board from Weir Pumps and shortly afterwards became first managing director and then chief executive of the Group in 1982. W. A. McLean, who had been brought into Weir Pumps to address the chronic industrial relation problems there, became the Group industrial relations director. He was well experienced in handling difficult situations, having been responsible for dealing with 'Red Robbo', the notorious chief shop steward at British Leyland's Longbridge plant. Sadly, in 1981 George Arkless died. As technical director of Weir Pumps he had made a great contribution in updating and improving designs, especially in the key area of boiler feed pumps. As already mentioned, Derald Ruttenberg joined the board in 1981.

There were further changes in the board in 1982. John Ferguson, who had been in charge of foundry operations at British Leyland, became an executive director in charge of the foundries. Bill Harkness, the company secretary, also joined the board. W. D. Coats, by then chairman of Coats Patons, retired. Two new non-executive directors were appointed – D. G. Milne, formerly chief executive of BP Oil, and R. D. Bertram, a partner in the well known Edinburgh lawyers, Dundas and Wilson. At the same time Francis Tombs indicated his intention to retire in April 1983.

The Group's return to profitability in 1981 was followed in 1982 by a year of consolidation in difficult market conditions. Most importantly of all, progress was made on the financial front. Net borrowings fell by £5 million, reflecting significant reductions in working capital. As a result of the improvement in cash flow, it was possible to dismantle the credit agreement made with the twelve banks in March 1981, and return to normal banking arrangements with the Royal Bank of Scotland and re-establish bonding facilities. The medium term loan agreements with FFI were also renegotiated and the term of the loans extended to 1994/98. The financial position would have been better still in 1982 if it had not been for delays in collecting a major debt due for the desalination plant which formed part of the aluminium smelter project in Dubai. Over £10 million was outstanding for well over a year. Eventually the debt was recovered when Margaret Thatcher intervened on Weir's behalf when she visited the Gulf. What was somewhat galling was the fact that, during the period it was unpaid, the ruling family had spent some $100 million on racehorses.

There were some interesting developments during the year. One was the introduction of a novel development, the down-hole pump for recovering oil from deep wells, particularly those at a high temperature. Electrically driven pumps were of course already in widespread use for this service, but as the wells were narrow in diameter the driving motors had to be very long to obtain the power needed, and the pumps needed many stages to generate the pressure required as their running speed could only be low. As a result they were unreliable, and indeed the motors often failed at higher temperatures. The Weir version was totally different. It was very compact and driven by a unique high-speed hydraulic turbine powered by either oil or water delivered from a high pressure pump on the surface. It ran at speeds up to 15,000 rpm, or ten times the speed of conventional pumps. As it was very small the designer could afford to make it in special corrosion and wear-resistant materials such as Stellite alloy. It was also used in geothermal service to maintain the groundwater pressure in geothermal wells, for example in the Unocal company's installation in California.

Desalination activities had by this time been relocated at Wokingham in the South of England, but no major contracts were won. The steel foundries still faced real difficulties from poor market conditions and overcapacity in the industry. A start was made, however, with a scheme managed by Lazards (although owing much to Weir's ideas), by which those choosing to remain in the industry contributed by a levy on sales to the closure costs of those foundries which saw no long-term future for themselves. Unfortunately, in spite of some progress in reducing capacity, the scheme never had the success it deserved – and that the industry so badly needed – due to the selfish attitude of two important foundry groups who decided not to join, but were happy to share in the benefits in spite of not contributing. However, the pattern and tooling business of the Group, G. Perry and Sons, enjoyed an excellent year in spite of the difficulties of the foundry industry generally.

Another unusual event in the year was the completion by Ayrshire Marine Constructors of the platform for the Maureen North Sea Oilfield of Phillips Petroleum. This giant structure, some 600 ft tall, was built at Hunterston in Ayrshire by Chicago Bridge and Iron, old friends of the Group, and Weir's had participated to give them some local Scottish connection and identity. Weir's contribution was limited to helping with relations with the Scottish Office and, more importantly, vetting labour recruitment to ensure that notable troublemakers from Clyde shipyards were not hired. On two occasions such folk actually tried to join under false names. It was an amazing construction feat. The main derrick lifted 400-ton prefabricated sections 600 feet in the air. Standing at the top of it, as the Weir board did one day, was a distinct challenge to those with the smallest touch of vertigo. One director, W. D. Coats, to his shame, did not even get up to the modest level where the lifting cage started. Weir's participation, although small, was fruitful and yielded a profit of £1 million.

Overall, the results for 1982, at £10 million profit before interest and tax, were £3 million lower than in 1981, although after tax they were virtually unchanged. 1983 was another year of consolidation. Trading conditions were difficult exacerbated by a decline in oil revenues, which affected important markets such as Nigeria and the Middle East. Weir Pumps not only faced severe competition, but also incurred additional costs on phasing out pump manufacture at the former Harland plant in Alloa. The steel foundries performed somewhat better than in the previous year, but faced very adverse market conditions.

During the year Francis Tombs retired as chairman. I replaced him. I should add that my secretary, Mrs Grieve, had loyally kept my visiting cards (which gave my title as 'Chairman') in the expectation that they would be needed again. John Young also retired, having made a very substantial contribution over many years, the latter part of the period having been particularly onerous. J. A. Lumsden retired as a non-executive director after 26 years on the board. Much effort was expended in both 1982 and 1983 on renegotiating the banking and loan agreements. In spite of the Group's evident recovery, this was not without some difficulty in the face of a sometimes unhelpful attitude from the banks. Eventually a reasonable settlement was achieved. Overall, the results for 1983 were disappointing, with profit before tax of £6.5 million, well down on the previous year. However, in the annual report, the chairman said that although the stance of the company over the two previous years had, of necessity, been almost wholly defensive, the company intended in the coming year to search for new activities as a start to shifting the balance of the business into areas where there were better growth prospects.

7

Ten years of growth
1984–93

In 1984 the Group took its first steps into new areas of business, as had been envisaged in the annual statement of the previous year. It was noticed that Vosper Thorneycroft, the shipbuilders and ship repairers, were in some difficulties and that they held, as legacy from a previous merger attempt, a 25 per cent stake in Yarrow's. Yarrow's had a distinguished history, both as the leading designer and builder of smaller warships and as a boilermaker. They had started life on the Thames, but had moved to Scotstoun on the Clyde at the end of the nineteenth century. Their shipbuilding business had been nationalised with grossly unfair and inadequate compensation, and the activities that remained primarily consisted of a company called YARD and a ticketing machine company. YARD was originally a co-operative venture between Yarrow's and the Royal Navy, and developed the designs for the propulsion machinery for each new class of warship. After nationalisation they became an engineering consultancy with a strong emphasis on marine and offshore oil work. Weir's believed that if they could purchase Vosper's 25 per cent stake, they would then be in a strong position to acquire Yarrow's and after disposing of the ticketing company would have YARD for a reasonable cost, and put into place ambitious plans for developing it.

Accordingly, through the good offices of Christopher Chataway (the MP and Olympic athlete), who had a friend on their board, Weir's were able to approach Vosper and purchase their holding for £3.5 million. In addition an agreement was made that if further compensation for nationalisation was forthcoming, Vosper's would be entitled to part of it. In the event, in spite of strenuous legal efforts by Yarrow's and Lithgow's (who had been similarly mistreated over compensation for their engine works) the Conservative Government, to their shame, and to the particular discredit of Keith Joseph, refused to remedy the injustice done. On a lighter note, as is often the case in such transactions, Weir's used a code word for Vosper. It was 'Vole', and the chairman of Vosper was delighted to find he was known as 'King Vole'. Christopher Chataway was rewarded for his help with a case of Cheval Blanc of an excellent vintage.

Weir's, however, did not bid for Yarrow's in 1984. Sir Eric Yarrow, their chairman, had been an apprentice at Weir's and the families had been friends for three generations, quite apart from a long business relationship, and I was unwilling to make a hostile bid while Sir Eric was chairman. After he retired in 1985, Weir's did make an offer, including an ingenious formula in the event of further compensation. It was not successful, and eventually after a great deal of negotiation with two rival buyers, Weir's sold their shareholding in 1986 to CAP (later to become CAP-Gemini) for £8.1 million, generating a very good profit.

When Francis Tombs had become chairman of Weir's, he had immediately dropped Rea Brothers as financial advisers and understandably, as he was a non-executive

director of theirs, would have liked to replace them perma-
nently by N. M. Rothschild. This would not have been
altogether an easy relationship, given Jacob Rothschild's
position as a major shareholder in Weir's and his break away
from the family bank. On Tombs's retirement, Morgan
Grenfell became Weir's merchant bank and provided excellent advice through Stephen Badger. Badger was a highly
intelligent, very amiable, but slightly eccentric executive.
He cycled to work at Great Winchester Street from distant
Dulwich come rain or shine. If some transaction was proposed, he would immediately put forward every sort of
argument against it, until he was eventually convinced of
its merits. In today's world, where transactions are so often
driven by considerations of fees and bonuses on the investment banking side, such behaviour is rare indeed. It is so
easily forgotten that at times the most valuable advice is not
to do something. As President Eisenhower was reputed to
have said to Secretary for State Foster Dulles, 'Don't just say
something, Foster. Stand there.'

Although 1984 was not an easy year, profit before tax
still rose strongly, from £4.9 million to £6.9 million. This
was an excellent result, given that continuing difficult
markets resulted in both the steel foundries and desalination making almost no profit contribution at all. Moreover,
early in the year there was a very serious strike at Cathcart
that lasted for five weeks. Ron Garrick confronted it in
very robust fashion, and the board went so far as to support
a threat (which was a serious one) of closing Cathcart. The
influence of the strikers' wives was of considerable effect in
persuading them to return to work.

In desalination, a major contract worth $50 million was
won for Ad Dur in Bahrain for a reverse-osmosis plant. The
project was a gift from Saudi Arabia to Bahrain, celebrating
the opening of the new causeway between the two

countries. The position of Bahrain, in terms of water supply, was rather different from other Gulf states. It had far more ground water than its neighbours, as could be seen by the numerous palm groves of that time. Apparently it was fed by an underground aquifer which originated in the mountains of Oman. Indeed it was actually possible to dive under the sea there and find fresh water bubbling up from the ocean bed. Nevertheless, a growing population and a higher standard of living meant that desalination was needed.

Another important initiative, which was related to the Group's strategy of building up service activities, was to separate, both physically and in management, the engineering business into Engineering Products and Engineering Services. Henceforth they were reported upon separately both in operational terms and in the annual report of the Group. The service centres of Weir Pumps at home and abroad were combined with those of Peacock Brothers in Canada in this new Services division, and in time other activities such as Weir Group Management Systems and oil drilling were added to it. Peter Syme, the managing director of Weir Pumps, moved over to head up Engineering Services, and John Hood, previously sales director at Weir Pumps, became its managing director.

Weir Group Management Systems started to develop significantly at this time, with £1 million of sales in 1984 to outside parties. The rationale behind the business was that as Weir's had a strong computer and information technology department, this activity could be expanded profitably to undertake work for others. Over time it grew and acquired similar service businesses, including one in the Midlands which serviced vegetable producers, and another, called Blackadder, provided support for Lloyd's underwriters.

There was further progress in 1985. Profits before tax increased by one third to £9 million. Gearing fell from 41

The *Jane Maersk*, a liquid gas carrier fitted with gas handling and storage equipment designed by Weir Liquid Gas Equipment in Edinburgh

A torpedo test installation at Strachan and Henshaw in Bristol

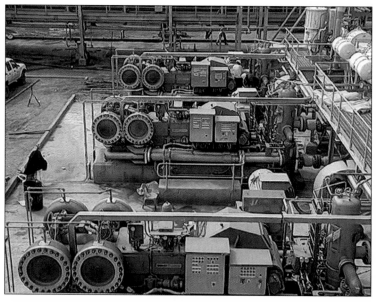

GEHO pumps at Murrin Murrin gold mine in Australia

Pilot operated safety relief valves supplied by Weir's French
valve company to Kozloduy power station in Bulgaria

Hydraulic power pumps for underground rock drills at the
Beatrix gold mine in South Africa

Concentrated sulphuric acid pump by Lewis Pumps, based in
St Louis, Missouri, and part of the Weir Group since 1994

EnviroTech scrubber pump for flue gas desulphurisation, now
marketed under the Warman name

Zeron™ alloy fittings from Weir Materials in Manchester

Boiler feed pump assembly at the Cathcart plant

Downhole gas/liquid handling pump for Texaco

The desalination plant built by Weir Westgarth at Jebel Ali,
Dubai, in the early 1990s, with a capacity of 60 million gallons
of fresh water a day

Hopkinson subsea ball valves

The AOD (argon oxygen decarburisation) furnace at the
Catton & Co. foundry, Leeds

A Warman 650HTP pump manufactured by Weir Minerals
South America being installed in early 2008 at a new tailings
line feeding the El Mauro dam in Chile

Atwood and Morrill 96-inch stainless steel Tricentric valve for
a wind tunnel at a United States Air Force base

per cent to 25 per cent, and by year end short term borrowings had virtually disappeared. By the end of the previous year over 70 per cent of the convertible preference shares had been converted into ordinary shares. Weir Pumps produced an excellent performance both in profits and in winning new orders. In boiler feed pumps they won their best market share ever. After a long period of difficult market conditions the steel foundries returned to profit. In France, Delas Weir continued to flourish and expand internationally. One highlight was the replacement of the main condenser at the Maine Yankee nuclear station in the USA. The 50 per cent share in Worthington Simpson was sold for £5.3 million to Dresser Industries. Derald Ruttenberg retired from the board during the year. He had given excellent advice as a director, but, far more importantly, he had played a key role in maintaining the independence of the Weir Group. Finally, during the year the forward strategy of the Group was set out in a more detailed and explicit form. It emphasised that service activity, including the servicing of equipment made by others, would be expanded; that there would be concentration on products which were of specialised design or involved specialist application engineering or manufacture; and that commodity products which mainly sold on price would be avoided. The rationale behind this two-pronged strategy was that the service business was not exposed to foreign competition; it was non-cyclical; there was an increasing demand for good class repair and maintenance facilities; there was a growth in outsourcing such operations by customers; and it produced attractive margins. In the case of engineering products it was clear that the UK was in general becoming a difficult place for manufacturing products where cost was all important and where there was a low degree of differentiation, and overseas competition was intense.

In the event, the following year was one of intense activity, and resulted in a major change in the structure of the Group. The steel foundries were sold to the firm of William Cook in Sheffield for £9.3 million in cash and an interest bearing note of £3.4 million. This transaction was done with somewhat mixed feelings, as the foundries had long been an integral part of the Group. In the 1970s they had been profitable, but more recently their performance had been affected by the cyclical nature of the industry and by over-capacity. A further important strategic consideration was the ongoing decline in the large part of their customer base represented by the UK engineering industry. The price received was approximately equal to the net assets of the foundries. There was an unfortunate sequel to the sale. Andrew Cook, the chairman of William Cook, was not by background a foundryman or engineer, but a solicitor. Whether this was a factor or not, he launched an action against Weir's not long after the sale in which, on various grounds such as misrepresentation, a sum greater than the purchase price paid was sought. Eventually this surprising and exceedingly optimistic claim was settled on the very much more modest basis of £500,000, not that any liability was admitted.

Since its formation, Delas Weir had produced excellent results every year, mainly on the back of the French nuclear power programme. In the previous five years the pre-tax profit attributable to Weir's 35 per cent share had averaged around £2.25 million each year. In Weir's hands, however, these profits were subject to a high level of tax, approaching 50 per cent. Nor were relations with Alsthom, the majority partner, always easy. Alsthom took an unconstructive view on the investment of the company's very large cash balances. They created difficulties about dividend payments and in truth probably resented the fact that the success of the business arose from the former Weiritam personnel who managed it and from Weiritam technology. Certainly this was not really a sound basis of partnership for going forward together in the longer term. Accordingly the Weir interest was sold to Alsthom for some £10 million. This was not a very generous price as, although it was twice Weir's share of the net assets of the business, it was a poor multiple of the company's solid earnings and little more than a pro-rata share of its cash holdings. Nevertheless it was a huge return on Weir's original investment of some £250,000 in the purchase of Weiritam, the predecessor company to Delas Weir.

As already recounted, the holding in Yarrow's was also sold in 1986. No doubt YARD would have been a good enough investment for Weir's in the longer term, but the price Yarrow shares had reached and at which Weir's sold out owed more to two rivals bidding against each other than to a rational valuation. During the year the government decided to privatise management of the operations of the naval dockyards at Rosyth and Devonport. Initially Weir's, in partnership with Balfour Beatty, bid against Babcock and Wilcox for Rosyth. Weir's lost, and it was humorously observed at the time that this result was inevitable. Babcock's bid (many copies of the documentation being required) needed a lorry to carry it, while Weir's bid needed only a small van. This loss was followed by a joint bid, this time in partnership with Balfour Beatty and the American firm of Brown and Root, for the much larger naval dockyard operation at Devonport, and early the following year it was announced that this was successful. Thus, Weir's gained at very modest cost a 30 per cent interest in the management of the Royal Navy's main maintenance and refitting capacity. It came with a host of listed historic buildings accompanied, however, by a less welcome host of antiquated working practices. The large prize to be won, either by Rosyth or Devonport, was the long-term programme of refitting the Royal Navy's nuclear submarine fleet, which at that time had not been decided, but was eventually to lead to a highly politicised contest.

Another acquisition was that of Tooling Products, a designer and manufacturer of tooling and moulds for the automotive industry. This may seem a somewhat unusual activity for Weir's, but it should be remembered that for many years they had owned G. Perry & Sons in Leicester, a leading maker of complex patterns for automotive foundries, and the two businesses had a considerable amount in common. Tooling Products' business was driven by the increasing use of plastics in cars in order to reduce weight and therefore improve fuel consumptions. Incidentally Jack Welch of General Electric had originally made his name in that firm by putting them into automotive plastics with great success. Although there was no mechanical engineering reason for high precision in most plastic car parts, an extremely high finish and dimensional accuracy was essential to give a good appearance on external parts. This in turn required very sophisticated machine tools, including electro-chemical machining, heavy investment, and a highly skilled workforce.

As a result of the various disposals, allied to a good operating performance, there was a strong cash generation of £23 million, even after the cost of acquisitions. The FFI loan of £10 million was paid off by a rights issue of one share for seven, and at year end there was no debt. It was certainly a dramatic change from the position a few years earlier. On the operating side of the business, Engineering Products performed well, particularly Weir Pumps, the highlights of their year being awards for £14 million of orders for the Sizewell B nuclear station and a large contract for the Daya Bay nuclear station in China. On a lesser scale, the turbo-drill was introduced with success in the North Sea by Weir Drilling, which had been formed two years earlier. Profit before tax, excluding any profit from disposals, improved from £9 million to £11.3 million.

In 1987, progress in developing the Group continued with the acquisition of Mather and Platt Machinery, which was purchased from the Wormald company of Australia for some £10 million. Mather and Platt was a long established competitor of Weir's, based in Manchester. Their headquarters and main plant was in that splendid Victorian building with a prominent clocktower which is familiar to many from the charming paintings of L. S. Lowry. Apart from pumps, Mather's also had a major business in fire-engineering. Wormald in fact had been a licensee of Mather's, and Mather's had almost bought it some years previously. Mather's had also been a leading manufacturer of textile machinery. Their chairman, Sir William Mather, recounted that in his father's time some Lancashire families, who were in the textile industry, would not have the Mathers in their houses because they had sold machinery to the nascent Indian cotton industry. An early and unusual example of non-tariff protectionism, one might say. Weir's and Mather's, as has previously been noted, negotiated abortively around 1970 to merge their pump interests, and Mather's had competed with Weir's to buy Harland Engineering.

When Wormald bid for Mather's, Sir William was ironically given the news of their action while he was staying with me to shoot grouse. He said he would not insult my intelligence by asking Weir's to become a 'white knight', as the price Wormald offered was so far in excess of the value of the business. Wormald, however, by a combination of poor and distant management, made a mess of the acquisition. Indeed, in the year to end June 1987, Mather and Platt Machinery had made a loss of almost £1 million. Weir's took energetic action once they had bought it, both to cut costs and integrate both manufacturing and service activities. Its product line was a good fit with Weir Pumps, as it filled gaps in the overall product range, in particular for larger water industry pumps and oil pipeline pumps. For example, in Iraq, almost every pumping station in the oil fields had been supplied by Mather's. (These were severely damaged years later by the RAF during the First Gulf War.) The acquisition also brought with it a foundry and heavy electric motor manufacture. Mather's had also developed in conjunction with Manchester University a special corrosion resistant alloy with the proprietary name of Zeron. This was later developed into a free-standing business of its own called Weir Materials. In the last quarter of the year the loss was turned around and a decent profit was earned.

Apart from this important acquisition, 1987 was a satisfactory year, with profit before tax and before exceptional items increasing from £11.3 million to £13.2 million. In spite of the cost of buying Mather's and of purchasing 4.4 per cent of the share capital of Howden's, the year ended with net cash of £10 million.

Howden's was a company which was in many ways a counterpart of Weir's, but instead of handling liquids, as Weir's did, it handled gases. Like Weir's, it was Glasgow based and had also been a family owned business for a comparable time. Just as Weir's made boiler feed-water heaters, so Howden made air heaters, and just as Weir's pumped water to boilers, so Howden pumped in heated air with its fans. Weir's pumped water from mines and Howden fans ventilated them, and just as Weir's made specialist pumps, so Howden made specialist compressors. As yet another example, in pressurised water reactors, Weir's made the pumps, and in gas cooled reactors Howden made the high performance gas circulators. There was plenty of sense in combining the two firms: obviously they had many customers in common, and their common technologies were in both fluid dynamics and heat exchange. Weir's had cash to spare and Howden's share price was very low, so they bought this stake. Jacob Rothschild's company joined them in buying an equivalent shareholding. Howden's were not interested in a merger, and Weir's were unwilling to make a hostile offer. When therefore, during the following year, the Howden share price rose sharply, Weir's disposal of their holding realised a profit of £2.5 million. Subsequently the Chartered Group bought Howden. Weir's were invited by Howden to intervene as a 'white knight', but declined.

Expansion of the Group continued in 1988, with the acquisitions of Liquid Gas Equipment Ltd, and of a 50 per cent interest in the turbo-drilling business of Neyrfor. Liquid Gas Equipment, or LGE, as it was known, was engaged as a process engineering contractor in the design and supply of the equipment involved in ships carrying liquid petroleum gases, or LPG, such as propane, butane and ethylene, and in shore installations. In addition to design and supply of the cargo handling and refrigeration systems, LGE also designed the cargo tanks, although the fabrication of these was often carried out by the shipyards involved. The scope of their supply amounted to as much as 50 per cent of the overall cost of the ship. LGE had originally been a part of Walter Runciman, the well-known shipowners. Its manager, and by that time owner, was a very entrepreneurial character, Jim Whyte, who also owned several gas carriers. By coincidence Weir's had been involved in the very early days of the LPG business. In the 1960s, recognising that Weir Westgarth's desalination business was inevitably very erratic – as there were not many contracts and they therefore tended to either be overloaded or have little work at all – and that their basic expertise was as process engineering contractors, Weir's had entered this field with some success. First of all they had designed and supplied the cargo equipment for two of the earlier LPG carriers, one in Spain and one with Hawthorn Leslie on the Tyne. They had also, for the main contractor, Chicago Bridge & Iron, carried out the same scope of work on land for a storage installation at the Fawley refinery of Esso, which was at the time the largest of its kind in the world. Weir Westgarth lost about £25,000 on a selling price of £1 million. This was not really a bad performance considering it was the first such land contract they had carried out and that work was much affected by bad weather. When Chicago Bridge were asked what they thought of Weir's financial result they surprisingly said it was excellent and that, on the first similar job they had done, their loss was the same as the selling price. J. R. Lang, however, who was Weir's managing director at the time, said he never wanted to hear the words LPG again. There was a certain irony, therefore, in Weir's re-entering the field.

The acquisition was a considerable success in the long term, but it was not without its dramatic moments. One contract was with an Italian shipyard and an Italian ship-owner, both rather fragile businesses. Almost simultaneously they both became virtually insolvent, with the ship only partly completed. Fortunately LGE kept title to their equipment until it was paid for. As a result, after exceedingly complicated negotiations, a consortium including Weir's and Jim Whyte ended up owning the ships, which were put under an Isle of Man company. By good fortune the freight rate for LPG eventually rose strongly, and they were able to dispose of the vessels. The financial outcome was therefore distinctly more favourable in the end than if the contract had been normally completed and paid for.

The other acquisition was the purchase of 50 per cent of the Neyrfor oil drilling business. Some time previously, Weir's had entered the turbo-drilling business, utilising the background technology they had developed for their down-hole pump, which was driven by a hydraulic turbine together with design concepts of Mitchell, an engineer from Aberdeen. Neyrfor was a subsidiary of Alsthom in France, and had independently developed a similar system, which was competitive with Weir's and rather more strongly established in the market. In conventional drilling the drill bit is driven by rotating the drill string (which is basically a long pipe) from the surface. In the turbo-drill the bit was attached to the hydraulic turbine, or to a lobe type drilling motor, powered by pumping fluid down from a high pressure pump on the surface. It was best suited for very deep or hot wells, but its real benefit was that by means of a sophisticated bearing system it could be steered. It was therefore invaluable when directional drilling, and even horizontal drilling, was required. It could moreover be steered very accurately. Some remarkable results were achieved, with the drill-bit finishing as much as three miles below the oil platform and three miles off in a lateral direction. The business was basically a rental one. Profits were somewhat erratic and clearly dependent on the state of exploration activity in the oil industry. Nevertheless it was a very satisfactory investment over the longer term. After eighteen months the balance of shares in Neyrfor were acquired from Alsthom. The business had initially been relocated from Grenoble to facilities in Aberdeen, from which it was managed.

A further small acquisition was the large-size pump business of W. H. Allen. It will be recalled that in 1970 they were the third party to the abortive merger with Mather and Platt and Weir's.

Financially the year was successful. Profits before tax increased by 35 per cent to almost £18 million. The dividend was raised substantially and £210 million of new orders were booked, with major successes in water pumping stations in the Middle East and for the London ring main project, and for boiler feed pumps in China, Poland and Australia. Unfortunately, no major desalination contract was won.

During the year Hugh Morrison became a non-executive director. This was an unusual appointment, as he was an under-secretary at the Industry Department for Scotland. In a rare and imaginative move by government, it was decided to give some civil servants more direct exposure to the realities of industrial life by seconding them for three years as unpaid outside directors of companies. Of course, when matters arose at meetings which affected relations with government, such directors left the room. He proved to be an excellent director. To the loss of government, he acquired a liking for the private sector and later became director of the Scotch Whisky Association, where he lobbied with great energy and success to protect the name and origin of Scotch against inferior and foreign imposter spirits. Kenneth Weir had encountered one of these as far back as 1929 when he had visited Japan. It bore the splendid composite name 'Black and White Horse'. On the label just such a noble animal was depicted, together with the fine slogan 'as drunk in Peers' Refreshment Room, House of Lords, England'. It was only equalled by the label on Chateau Lion, a native Japanese red wine of doubtful flavour. That showed a lion, very similar to the beast used as trademark by MGM Films, and the charming words 'put in his bottle in my cave'.

The major event in 1989 was the purchase of Hopkinson's, the renowned valve makers in Huddersfield. The Group had earlier, and unsuccessfully, entered the valve industry through Weir-Pacific Valves. In spite of the failure of that effort, which had been due to the Group's own shortcomings, the industry remained an attractive looking one. The customers were much the same, and both pumps and valves were used together in the fluid technology field. This acquisition was not an opportunistic move, but one which had been in the mind of Weir's management for some time. Indeed they were very familiar with Hopkinson's products, not only as users, but also as Hopkinson's sales agents in Canada through Peacock Brothers.

Hopkinson's were established in the nineteenth century and made their name as inventors of the first reliable safety valves for boilers, at a time when steam pressures were rising and boiler explosions were sadly frequent and disastrous events. They followed that by taking a licence from Ferranti, a famous early pioneer in the electrical industry, who had patented the venturi valve. This ingenious design both recovered the pressure loss when steam passed through the valve but also reduced the size of the valve and the force needed to open or shut it. Hopkinson's had built up a highly successful business over the years and also had product lines in control valves, valve actuators and soot blowers for cleaning boilers. They had, however, become a somewhat complacent and ossified business with little investment in modern machine tools and a poor reputation for deliveries, which had opened the door for competitors. Nevertheless their product and their name were excellent ones. At this time they had serious and intractable industrial relations problems. This led to their board taking the highly unusual step of advertising in the financial press that the business was up for sale.

Weir's therefore acquired it together with an option to purchase Atwood and Morrill Inc., an equivalent business based in Salem in the USA. Atwood and Morrill had a particularly good position in the nuclear industry, one product being their main steam isolating valve. These huge valves had a key safety role in shutting off in emergency the steam generated by the reactor and doing so in a couple of seconds. They also licensed these products outside the USA. Indeed, Delas Weir were licensees in France, and had supplied their isolating valves to virtually all the stations in the large French nuclear programme. In Salem (famous for its witch-burning activities in the seventeenth century), Atwood and Morrill occupied the former premises of the Stanley Steam-car Company, whose nameplate remained in place above their entrance. The 1st Lord Weir had, when driving his Darracq in his motor racing days, been very proud of having defeated Mr Stanley himself in the RAC hill climbing competition.

Hopkinson's had been losing money up to their acquisition by Weir's, due in part to their very poor labour relations. Within a few months, energetic action by Bill McLean restored them to profit. A substantial programme was put in hand to install modern machine tools, reorganise their factory layout and improve their steel foundry.

There was further progress in 1990. Profits before exceptional items and tax rose strongly from £20 million to over £27 million, with both Engineering Products and Services making an increased contribution. The highlight of the year was the acquisition of Strachan and Henshaw, specialist engineers based in Bristol. They belonged to the Dickinson Robinson Group, who were not only manufacturers of paper products, particularly well known for their stationery, but also had large interests in packaging, for which Strachan and Henshaw made machinery. Dickinson Robinson had been taken over by a financial raider company called Pembridge, with the objective of breaking it up. The opportunity therefore arose for Weir's to acquire the Strachan and Henshaw business, other than the packaging machinery interests.

Its activities certainly fitted in with Weir's strategy of concentrating on specialist engineering. In the nuclear field, Strachan and Henshaw designed and built highly sophisticated devices for the remote handling of nuclear fuel, for example in storage pools, and the huge refuelling machines for gas-cooled reactors. They were a major supplier to the Royal Navy and to foreign navies of underwater weapon launching systems, including torpedo tubes and torpedo handling gear, and had a facility in Bristol for test firing torpedoes. Weir's were already involved in this aspect of their business, as they had developed the air-turbine pump for torpedo launching. This ingenious device propelled the torpedo out of the tube with a bolt of high pressure water, rather than the traditional use of compressed air. It made it much harder for an opposing boat to hear the launch of the weapons. At an earlier date I had in fact asked Sir John Miln, the chairman of Dickinson Robinson, if he would sell Strachan and Henshaw, but had been turned down. Other activities, all basically connected with complex handling, were stacker-reclaimers for coal and mineral ores and equipment for unloading and loading coal between rail cars and ships. Notable coal ports such as Hampton Roads in the United States, Richards Bay in South Africa and Robert's Bank in British Colombia had been equipped by them.

Accordingly Weir's purchased the business for £30.5 million from Pembridge. However, Strachan and Henshaw held, after Pembridge had repaid loans, cash of £27.5 million. The Ministry of Defence and the bank who had issued performance bonds fortunately insisted that the cash in Strachan and Henshaw should effectively be ring-fenced, so that Pembridge could not gain access to it. Of course some of the cash was genuinely advance payments, but a substantial part was simply the result of an ultra-conservative policy for taking profits. Thus, in financial terms, the acquisition was a cheap one for Weir's, particularly as Strachan and Henshaw's profit for 1989 on a pro-forma basis was £6.66 million before tax. Their order book was £119 million and included a large long term order from the Royal Australian Navy for the weapon system for their programme of Collins class submarines.

The other acquisition was the exercise, for £8 million in cash, of the option to acquire Atwood and Morrill, which had been arranged as part of the purchase of Hopkinson's. In order to finance these two transactions a rights issue of 12 million new shares was made at a price of 250p per share and on the basis of one new share for every five shares held. At the same time the assets of Strachan and Henshaw were revalued, and application was made to the courts to reduce the Group's share premium account so as to write off the balance of goodwill which had arisen.

During the year, in spite of the good trading results, problems began to emerge at the Ad Dur desalination plant being built in Bahrain. These were eventually to lead to very serious losses. Although these were never specifically identified in the Group's annual report and accounts, they amounted over the period of the contract to no less than £12 million. The cost had indeed been underestimated, and later on technical problems were also to bedevil the project. The worst problem, however, was that the consulting engineer insisted on changes which meant that he got a plant of the design he wanted rather than the one which had been specified and for which Weir's had tendered. To make matters more difficult, the fact that the plant was a present from Saudi Arabia to Bahrain, and that it was late in delivery, had diplomatic implications.

In 1991 there were changes in the board. Alistair Fleming, previously managing director (construction) of Eurotunnel, joined as an executive director taking overall responsibility for Weir Westgarth, Liquid Gas Equipment and Strachan and Henshaw, and Jean de Raemy retired. Howard Macdonald, formerly treasurer of Royal Dutch/Shell and chief executive of Dome Petroleum, joined as a non-executive, and Denys Milne retired.

It was a year of recession and widespread economic difficulty. It was therefore very encouraging that profits before tax increased by 26 per cent to £34.2 million. New orders at almost £500 million increased strongly across the Group. After a number of years without major contracts Weir Westgarth secured a £70 million order for the Jebel Ali 'G' desalination plant in Dubai, forming part of a power and water scheme for which the gas turbine power station was supplied by Siemens. The plant was built in partnership with Belleli SpA of Italy, who supplied the main fabrication from their shops in Saudi Arabia, and with whom Weir's had now worked for 25 years.

In 1990, Weir's had established a foothold in the valve industry in the USA through the purchase of Atwood and Morrill. In 1991 they acquired for the first time a US pump manufacturer in the shape of Floway, based in Fresno, California. Fresno was in the Imperial Valley, a prolific agricultural district, and styled itself 'the Lettuce Capital of the World'. Indeed it was surrounded by thousands of acres of the stuff from farms producing several crops in the year. The raison d'être of Floway had been as a supplier of vertical irrigation pumps for local agriculture, and they had developed from that into a whole range of vertical pumps for many applications. It was a good, sound business and well managed. Somewhat remarkably, it regularly sold large numbers of irrigation pumps to Saudi Arabia. In spite of negligible rainfall and conventional water resources which had resulted in the extensive construction of desalination plants, some parts of Saudi Arabia had substantial deposits of what is sometimes called 'mined water'. These are underground reservoirs of water which has been trapped for many millions of years. It is not renewable (obviously, as there is no rainfall), but it can be pumped up and used, once and for all, for irrigation. This the Saudi government did, thus giving stability and an occupation to previously nomadic tribes. In some years over a million tons of wheat were grown, and although it was not economic it was as sensible a use as any for a small part of the country's vast oil revenue, and certainly more sensible than some.

The acquisition of Floway brought Weir's into contact with some of California's distinctive environmental legislation, in this case legislation relating to ground water pollution. The previous occupants of the Floway site had been a slot machine manufacturer and an oil company. The former had allowed a degreasing chemical, carbon tetra-fluoride, to leak into the ground. The oil company had leaking storage tanks, thus bringing their past operations under the jurisdiction of LUST (or 'Leaking Underground Storage Tank') legislation. The laws in California on water table pollution are strict. In some cases they are also absurd, because when the legislation was debated, politicians, in their attempts to appear greener and cleaner than their rivals, kept reducing the allowable limits for some chemicals until they were below the level at which they could actually be measured by any commercially available instrumentation. In any event, Weir's had to put in a ground water remediation programme, to which the previous occupants contributed and which continues to this day at substantial cost. Happily the lettuce around Fresno is still as nice looking, tasteless and abundant as ever.

The Floway transaction had been brought to Weir's by Erskine Bowles, an investment banker in the Carolinas. Subsequently he became well known publicly as chief of staff to President Clinton. Incidentally the transaction took longer to finalise than expected. On the legal side, Weir's were represented by Marilyn Sobel, of the New York firm of Paul Weiss. Her opposite number was another lady lawyer, and neither was prepared, as a matter of pride, to concede even a comma to the other.

Floway was not Weir's only attempt to enter the US pump market: other attempts had been made previously, and many others were to be made in the future. In some cases there had been nothing more than a quick look and analysis and rejection of the idea. In others, serious formal bids had been made.

It might reasonably be asked why there seemed to be a good number of pump businesses for sale in the USA. The reason was fairly clear. The stock market is often a driver of American industry. Some readers, without being unduly cynical, might think this was the wrong way around, and that the stock market was originally supposed to be an innovative and effective means of raising capital for industry, rather than a way of telling industry what it ought not to do. So be it, but the reality was that the stock market had decided that pumps (and a lot of other widely needed essential products, even those with certain and inherent growth in demand) were 'rust-belt'. As a matter of fact, if you did try to manufacture them in the traditional 'rust-belt' – being those Eastern states which were first industrialised – it was quite difficult, as you were likely to be in the territory of the United Steelworkers union. They covered much of the engineering industry and imposed high wage rates, retirement and medical benefits. These conditions were derived from earlier days when the American steel industry itself had been dominant and highly profitable, but which were completely unrealistic in the latter part of the twentieth century. Moreover, it can fairly be said that being friendless in the capital markets, the older established engineering industries in the United States had not only failed to attract the investment needed in modern equipment, but they had also failed in most cases to attract good enough management. Of course, those who had invested, insisted on strong management and technical excellence, and taken a progressive view, had prospered greatly. For example, while US competitors fell by the wayside and disappeared, General Electric prospered in the power station turbine business – whether steam or gas turbine – making a superior return on capital and on sales, and was quite able to beat foreign competitors even from countries with much lower wage rates. So there were certainly opportunities in the USA.

While Floway was the first acquisition of a US pump maker which the Group had made, Weir's had looked at a number of other possibilities there, as they believed they must build up a much stronger presence in the US pump market. Earlier, a serious attempt was made to purchase the Byron Jackson companies. These consisted of Byron Jackson Pumps, Borg Warner Seals and a business making actuators for guiding military missiles. The pump company was long established in the oil business, where it was, together with Pacific Pumps, considered one of the top class makers. It was also active in the boiler-feed pump and nuclear reactor circulating pump markets. Clearly, therefore, it was an excellent fit for Weir's. The seal business manufactured sophisticated mechanical seals for pumps and compressors.

The owners, Borg Warner, were active primarily in the automobile industry, being best known for their automatic transmission systems, and they sold off these other subsidiaries to raise cash and to concentrate on their core activities. The pump company had however been somewhat neglected. It was not well managed and needed capital investment and rationalisation of its facilities. In addition it had been backward in providing proper servicing for its products. Weir's therefore saw considerable potential for improvement and for substantial benefits from synergies.

The sale process was complicated and time consuming. It brought Weir's for the first time into contact with US corporate lawyers and their (at least to Scots) huge fees. In this connection, Derald Ruttenberg's family company, Tinicum, kindly gave great assistance to Weir's, effectively acting as their financial adviser. Weir's had only been prepared to embark on it at all on the assurance from J. P. Morgan, who were handling the sale for Borg Warner, that they were not competing with a management buy-out. In the end, to Weir's considerable disappointment, the companies were acquired by Clayton Dubilier, a private equity house, with the active participation of the Byron Jackson management. Strictly speaking, perhaps it was not a management buy-out, but it certainly was very close to one, and Weir's had every right to feel distinctly aggrieved at the whole episode.

Among other pump companies which Weir's investigated around this time with a view to acquisition were Romec, a maker of aircraft engine fuel pumps. They were, however, dependent to a considerable degree on customers in the private aircraft sector, such as Cessna and Piper, and such businesses were in difficulties as their market was adversely affected by the high cost of third party insurance for private aircraft owners. Two other opportunities were missed because the asking price seemed to Weir's to be too high; these were Mono Pumps, who made progressing-cavity pumps used in the process industries, and Johnson, a leading US maker of vertical pumps. Negotiations to buy Hazelton Pumps, a family owned business in Pennsylvania, reached a very advanced state. When Weir's carried out a due diligence exercise, however, they called off completion of the purchase on discovering that the potential unfunded liability for retirees medical expenses was very high, and the owners had been apparently unaware of this when setting the asking price. Some years later, though, Hazelton joined the Group as part of the purchase of Warman.

Two other major acquisitions which were considered were SIHI-Halberg in Germany, and the pump division of Sulzer in Switzerland. In neither case was it possible to reach agreement. Acquisition of Sulzer would have been a major step forward. Sulzer was Weir's main competitor in the boiler-feed pump market, and a combination of the two, who between them had the best design technology in the business, would have made a formidable and dominant worldwide force. Sulzer were also competitors in high pressure pumps for the oil industry and water supply pumps and had an international network which would have fitted very well with Weir's. A smaller acquisition in Germany, in the shape of Allweiler, who made screw-pumps, was also investigated, but again turned down.

In 1992, the main acquisition was Darchem Engineering. This was a part of the Darlington group of companies, who were a subsidiary of William Baird and whose main activity was in conventional insulation. Darchem Engineering, however, specialised in metallic insulation, which was used in cladding nuclear reactor vessels. The insulation was made from thin stainless steel sheeting which was formed by a sophisticated process into something best described as a metal honeycomb. The advantage was that in the event of radioactive leakage it could, unlike conventional insulation, be decontaminated by being washed down with water. The manufacturing process, which included shaping honeycomb material very accurately by cutting with lasers, also enabled Darchem to make lightweight titanium shapes for the internal core of jet-engine compressor blades for Rolls Royce and similar complex applications such as the air-guidance system for wind tunnels supplied to customers such as Boeing and NASA in America. Other activities were all related to heat and fire and included fire testing facilities. In these, for example, prototypes of the rolling stock for the Channel Tunnel were tested under actual fire conditions. In addition they operated a substantial business in heat-treating components, such as automobile engine valves, for third parties. Their most important activity in time became that of manufacturing highly specialised components for aircraft, such as fire protection barriers on aircraft engines, and they even made fire-proof containers for the 'black boxes' recording key data in aircraft in the event of a crash. As it turned out, the lack of an ongoing UK nuclear reactor programme meant eventually that they never fulfilled their real potential, although they did sell some metallic insulation for reactors in Japan and in France.

There was a highly contentious episode in 1993. This was the award of the programme for maintaining, refitting and refuelling the Royal Navy's Vanguard nuclear submarine fleet. The choice lay between Rosyth Dockyard, which was operated by Babcock and Wilcox, and Devonport, operated by a consortium of Weir's, Balfour Beatty, and Brown and Root. It was a highly politicised affair. In one corner was the Scottish Office, arguing for Rosyth, and in the other West Country MPs such as Tom King, who had

been Defence Secretary until 1992. The issue was complicated by the fact that work on the new dock which would
have been needed at Rosyth had been started, but then
suspended. The Devonport consortium put in an unsolic-
ited bid. As can be imagined, every politician and every
journalist in Scotland had his shout, but in the event the
decision went in Devonport's favour and design work
started on the very complicated dock and refuelling facility.
Negotiations for the purchase of the dockyard – rather than
simply managing it – were started, but dragged on for two
years. Because of nuclear fuel handling, the Nuclear Inspec-
torate naturally became involved. Esoteric questions were
raised, such as what would happen if an aircraft crashed on
the facility while a submarine was being refuelled? Much
time was wasted, and the cost of the project greatly increased,
with no significant increase in safety. It is no wonder that
nuclear power in the UK has been a poor relation to the
industry in France.

This chapter has so far mainly been concerned with the
acquisitions which were made over this ten-year period.
These acquisitions were to change the shape of the Group
fundamentally. During this time, however, the Group grew
strongly both in size and in its profits, not simply as a result
of these acquisitions, but also from steady organic growth
arising from its existing businesses. Some account is therefore necessary of the operations of the various companies
and of the consequent results in financial terms during this
period.

In 1984, the foundries were affected by the coal miners'
strike, which disrupted electricity supplies, and this resulted
in the loss of some 1,000 tonnes of castings output. The
down-hole pump was successfully introduced in the North
Sea oil fields with orders for the Auk, Forties, and Ninian
fields, one unit being installed at a depth of 8,000 feet. The

following year saw many successes for Weir Pumps in the power station field, with orders in India, the Far East and the USA, and the best market share for boiler feed pumps for many years. In Engineering Services, apart from the UK, there were now service centres in the Netherlands, Dubai, Saudi Arabia and Oman, and in Canada, Peacock's were now operating such centres in Montreal, Toronto, Calgary and Edmonton. In 1985, the steel foundries recovered from the previous year's setback and provided an operating profit of £1.8 million, although this represented a sales margin of only some 5 per cent. The Lazard scheme for foundry rationalisation had been of some help, albeit limited.

The highlight of 1986 was the decision, after the interminable Layfield enquiry, to proceed with the pressurised water reactor for Sizewell B. The importance of this to the Group, in terms of orders for pumps, valves and test equipment, can be seen from the initial orders of £14 million placed that year. In subsequent years this was substantially increased. In this year the two-phase pump to handle oil and gas mixtures was ordered for the first time. During the next two years, exploration drilling was carried out extensively in the Qatar North Dome, which would subsequently turn out to be one of the largest gas reserves in the world. Further large boiler feed pump orders followed in China, Poland and Australia. In the water supply and sewage handling market there were major contracts for Kaduna in Nigeria, and other projects in Africa and the Middle East, and the first of several orders was awarded for the massive London ring-main project. When completed, the cost of this massive water pipeline which encircles London was actually greater than the cost of the Channel Tunnel. As far as the latter was concerned, it emerged that it was beyond the capability of the local water authority to supply the fresh water needed by the tunnel contractors, and accordingly Weir Westgarth provided a desalination plant. Over this period Weir Material Services steadily built up their business in the highly corrosion resistant Zeron material, many applications being for the offshore oil industry.

Weir Pumps had a banner year in 1990. New orders booked reached the record figure of £164 million, with a particularly good performance in the North Sea with contracts for the Bruce, Brae, Tiffany, Nelson and Scott oil fields. Weir Pumps followed this with another good year in 1991. The highlight, however, was Weir Westgarth's £70 million contract in Dubai for the Jebel Ali desalination plant. Weir Westgarth also were awarded an interesting contract in the North Sea for a sulphate removal plant which treated 100,000 barrels of sea water per day for injection into oil wells. As far as service business was concerned, contracts were won to refurbish three water pumping stations in Kuwait which had been damaged in the Gulf War, and similar work was subsequently undertaken on desalination plants. LGE was very active, winning nine orders for gas carrying ships in the UK, Italy and Korea, and commissioning and handing over to their owners eight other ships. Strachan and Henshaw won further work on underwater weapon launching systems for submarines of the Royal Navy and Royal Australian Navy, and several major bulk material handling installations in Bristol, China, India and the USA.

Highlights of 1992 were feed pump orders for three reactors at Wolsong in South Korea and a £12 million order in China for similar equipment. Substantial orders for pumps and valves were won for a number of combined-cycle power stations in the UK and yet more work obtained on the London ring main. There was another major desalination contract in 1993, this time in Qatar, for £80 million, in partnership with Asea Brown Boveri. Incidentally, these large desalination plants also provided many orders for pumps and valves to Weir Pumps and Hopkinson's.

As this chapter covers the ten years from 1984 when the Group embarked on an explicit strategy of growth, it is relevant at this point to judge the extent to which this ambition was achieved. Turnover grew from £131 million to £450 million, a substantial rise even allowing for inflation. Profit before tax increased from £6.8 million to £34.2 million and earnings per share from 2.8p to 18.3p per share, while dividends rose from 1.25p to 6.5p per share. As far as the balance sheet was concerned, shareholders' funds were £46 million in 1984 and £125 million by end 1993. In 1984, debt in the shape of loan capital and bank loans stood at £19.5 million, offset by a small amount of cash, whereas in 1993, after offsetting borrowings, the Group held £54 million in cash or cash equivalents. In financial terms, therefore, the objective of growth had certainly been achieved.

Clearly the shareholders benefited considerably from this progress. While it is not very common to find several shareholders each holding 10 per cent of a public company, in Weir's case, in 1990 for example, Schroder's, the Prudential and M&G between them held over 35 per cent. They were not the only beneficiaries. Employees who had joined the Save As You Earn option scheme when Weir's shares were at their nadir also did very well.

The strategy pursued was to develop in specialist engineering products and at the same time increase the Group's involvement in engineering services. In 1984 Engineering Services reported turnover (including the Group's share of associate companies) at £32 million, on which a trading profit of £2.76 million was made. The comparable figures for 1993 were £175 million of turnover and £12.3 million profit. Over the same period, the results for Engineering Products were a growth in turnover from £102 million to £361 million, and in profit from £6.23 million to £25.6 million.

The target of expanding Engineering Services had therefore certainly been met. As to Engineering Products, the Group had also stuck to its strategy of concentrating on specialist activities, whether by way of the acquisitions it had made or by internal product development. Certainly the Group could not be called a conglomerate. It is worth remarking, however, that, apart from Floway and Hopkinson's, the other acquisitions were outside the fields in which the Group had traditionally operated. It would of course have been ideal if there had been better opportunities to expand the pump business. The Group, at least for most of the period, certainly had the financial capacity to have done so, and it was not for want of trying that they did not succeed. In the next chapter we will see how a major such opportunity arose and was taken, and which was eventually to shift the balance of the Group in the longer term.

8

Towards the present
1994–2002

In 1994, as for several years previously, the Group's report and accounts showed separately the contributions in turn-over and profits of Engineering Products and Engineering Services. The narrative also covered developments and activities in five main markets: power; oil and gas; water and sewage; naval and marine; and general industrial. This diversity was certainly considered an important strength, although Ron Garrick and I sometimes said to each other, not entirely in jest, that we hoped we would not see a year when every single one of the markets was strong, as the following year would inevitably be a poorer one.

The markets were not of equal importance, however. The share of new orders won by naval and marine in 1993 and 1994 was 6 per cent and 7 per cent respectively, although in fairness this did not include the Group's pro-rata share of Dev-onport dockyard's naval business. Moreover a very large pro-portion of work in this market was represented either by contracts at Weir Pumps and Strachan and Henshaw for sub-marine programmes or at LGE for shipboard liquid gas han-dling contracts. Very little indeed was for merchant shipping.

For almost thirty years after the Second World War, supplying equipment for commercial ship owners had been a core part of Weir's business. Of course there were unfavourable external factors. British shipbuilding effectively collapsed after some years due to uncompetitive costs, and continental yards eventually moved in the same direction. British ship owners no longer enjoyed a predominant position, as a result of the much reduced UK share of world trade and competition from foreign owners who sailed under flags of convenience and paid no taxes. In the tanker market the British owners Shell and BP, who specified the equipment on their ships, relied to a lesser extent than before on their own fleets, and passenger liners had given way to air travel. This is not to say that people had stopped building ships, though. Far from it: shipbuilding had grown rapidly in Japan, closely followed by South Korea, and later by lesser new arrivals such as Brazil. The fact was that Weir's – despite recovering their position in the power and water markets by improved design and manufacturing efficiency, and making a good entry into oil and gas – had lost their place in the merchant shipbuilding market. It would not have been easy to keep it. The Japanese yards, for example, strongly favoured using local suppliers such as Shenko and Ebarra to maintain the low prices for their ships, whereas in former times individual ship owners could more easily specify equipment of their choice. Nevertheless Hamworthy, a UK competitor of Weir's, certainly continued to have more success than Weir's in this challenging and large market.

It would clearly therefore have been of great benefit to Weir's to find a major new pump market to replace the one they had lost, even if it cannot in truth be said that they had specifically identified this shortcoming. Such an opportunity arose in 1994 in the shape of EnviroTech Pump

Systems. Twenty-five years earlier the acquisition of Harland Engineering had been a vital step in Weir's re-establishing itself as a leader in the UK pump industry. The acquisition of EnviroTech was equally significant as the first step in putting the company in a position to become a truly international force.

EnviroTech was a pump group and was therefore not a core activity for Baker Hughes, to whom it belonged, and whose main business was in the oil industry. Its headquarters were in Salt Lake City in Utah, traditionally an important centre for the US mining industry. Much of the business covered the supply of pumps handling abrasive and aggressive fluids, including slurries with a high solids content, and applications included piping systems for transporting these, as well as such services as mill circuit pumps and the disposal of mine tailings. Other parts of the EnviroTech group included Lewis Pumps based in St Louis, the GEHO and Begemann companies in Holland, and the Vulco companies in Chile. Lewis Pumps was a very specialist business producing pumps and valves for handling highly corrosive acids used in many parts of the mining industry. Lewis had expertise in proprietary acid-resistant alloys, and, given the essential duties its equipment provided, a first class and very rapid spare parts service was provided to customers worldwide. GEHO manufactured a range of positive-displacement diaphragm pumps of unique design for handling liquids containing larger sized solids. Vulco provided local manufacture and servicing for the extensive mining industry in Chile and other South American countries. It also had, as did Salt Lake City, facilities for rubber lining of pumps, piping and allied equipment. Due to the rugged service conditions of much of its equipment, EnviroTech generated a substantial after-market in spares and service. Given EnviroTech's location in the Mormon epicentre of

Salt Lake City, it was no surprise that many of its people were of the Mormon faith. To their natural personal qualities of diligence and hard work they added, as a result of their experience as overseas missionaries for their Church, ability in many foreign languages.

Slurry handling was not in fact unfamiliar to Weir's by 1994, as they had themselves successfully developed hard-wearing pumps for very demanding applications in flue-gas desulphurisation systems, demand for which had grown to reduce sulphur dioxide emissions from coal fired power stations – a principal cause of harmful acid rain.

The acquisition of EnviroTech was financed by a rights issue of one new share for every four held at a price of 252p per share, underwritten by Morgan Grenfell, and the balance by cash from Weir's own resources. At the time of the acquisition a provision of £7.8 million was made for reorganisation costs. From the start, EnviroTech made a positive contribution to the earnings of the Group. Prior to the acquisition of EnviroTech, pumps had represented 40 per cent of the Group's turnover, although this figure should be judged in the context of the substantial element of contracting rather than manufacturing carried out by such subsidiaries as Weir Westgarth. The addition of Envirotech had the significant effect of increasing the share of pump business to 55 per cent of the total.

During 1994 there were changes to the Group's board. David Dunbar, formerly finance director of Brown and Root, joined with special responsibility for business development. At the same time Bill McLean retired. He had been a director since 1981 and had been responsible for human resources and industrial relations during that time.

Results for the year were largely unchanged from 1993. Weir Pumps, Hopkinson's and Atwood and Morrill won important orders in the Far East, for three nuclear plants in

Korea; and for several new power stations in Indonesia, Singapore, Malaysia and China. Strachan and Henshaw won a major order for coal handling equipment in China.

Neyrfor Weir also had an excellent year, which included much drilling work in Qatar in what was eventually to become one of the most important natural gas fields in the world – so large, indeed, that at one time linking it to European markets by direct pipeline was considered. Weir Materials won a most unusual order worth over £4 million for Zeron 100 material to line part of the new Jubilee Line tunnel for London Underground, which was exposed to attack from aggressive organic acids in the soil.

At Devonport a start was made to what were to prove protracted and difficult negotiations for Weir's and their partners to purchase the dockyard rather than simply manage it.

The acquisition of EnviroTech resulted in the Americas becoming the Group's most important market for the first time in 1995. The increased penetration of Far East markets, particularly for power station work, and the Group's established presence in the Middle East put those markets in total not far behind the UK. Thus the wider balance of markets, both by geography and industry, which Weir's for some time had sought to obtain, became a reality.

It was a successful year and profits before tax reached a new record of £45 million. The intake of new orders at £640 million was some 40 per cent higher than the previous year. No large contracts, such as desalination plant, were included, which made this figure all the more encouraging. Indeed the largest single order was £20 million, which Weir Pumps and the valve companies won for the Quinshan nuclear power station in China. Another development was a dramatic change in policy by major Japanese power station contractors, notably Mitsubishi Heavy Industries.

Previously these firms had invariably insisted on using Japanese suppliers. As a result of the strength of their currency, they now liberalised their purchasing policy in order to remain competitive, and as a result Weir's benefited from substantial orders in Pakistan, Taiwan, Thailand, Indonesia and Malaysia. Even in Japan itself Darchem won two orders for metallic insulation on nuclear reactors being built for Tokyo Electric Power, the world's largest utility company. (As a footnote to the business won from Mitsubishi, it is of interest to note that a hundred years previously, Mitsubishi had become a licensee for Weir's marine equipment.)

One order won by Strachan and Henshaw was most unusual. Russia was falling behind in the programme to decommission nuclear warheads that had been agreed with the USA, apparently – if unbelievably – because they simply did not have suitable containers in which to safely transport them. Strachan and Henshaw therefore, in conjunction with GKN, were awarded a contract for £12 million to supply special containers. The specification for these demanded that they could withstand a most unusual test procedure which consisted of firing high-powered bullets, presumably to ensure they could survive an attack by terrorists. The traditional side of Strachan and Henshaw also undertook a programme for the Royal Navy to adapt nuclear submarines so that they could handle and launch cruise missiles, as they later did during the Iraq conflicts.

A diversification made during the year into a completely new engineering services field was the acquisition of 24 per cent of the equity and 50 per cent of the preference shares, for some £6 million, in First Engineering, a newly privatised rail maintenance operation covering most of the track operated by ScotRail.

There were two changes among the executive directors. Alistair Fleming resigned in order to become chief executive of Forth Ports, and Kevin Gamble joined the Group from Senior Engineering, taking on responsibility for Strachan and Henshaw and a number of other companies, as well as for overseeing personnel matters.

The following year, 1996, was fairly uneventful. There were no very large contracts won, but most parts of the Group performed well, with further success in the Far East power market. Profits before tax increased again to £49 million. Strachan and Henshaw's profits had been dragged down in previous years by their involvement as erection contractors, involving as this did disputes over the scope of work, but it was in any event a low margin business and accordingly this activity was discontinued. Ian Percy, formerly senior partner of Grant Thornton and a doyen of the accounting profession, joined the board. He took the place of Duncan MacLeod, who had been a director for twenty years, and thus gave the board the continuity of having a distinguished accountant as an independent director, an important support for the Group finance director, Ian Boyd.

One very interesting product development was that of the mixed flow pump. This was the solution to a uniquely challenging problem. Most oil wells produce a mixture of oil and gas, and in the North Sea, for example, much of the plant on an oil platform is involved in separation of the two. Platform design would be greatly simplified and costs reduced if a method could be found to pump the mixture directly onshore. There were two main problems facing the designer. The first was that the proportions of oil and gas can vary, from all oil at one extreme to all gas at the other. The second was that oil, like water, cannot be compressed, whereas gas can be. Clearly the normal design parameters therefore do not apply. Another problem was a commercial one. In principle such a machine could save millions in capital expenditure, but it was expensive to develop and if Weir's had been able to afford the research and development programme on their own account (and there was always a large risk that they might not find a solution), then they could hardly price the machine at a level which would recover the development cost. The solution was to engage several major oil companies as partners. They each put up an initial payment, on the understanding that if the first stage of development work achieved a predetermined goal, then they would subscribe further funds to complete the work. In the event an ingenious solution was found, and the first unit was ordered for the Captain field of Texaco.

In 1997 my forthcoming retirement, at the end of January 1998 after over forty years with the Group, was announced. It was in fact 48 years in total, if I count working as a sixteen-year-old apprentice during my summer holidays from school at Eton, when I was paid the princely wage of one pound and seven shillings a week, the going rate at that time. Sir Ron Garrick was to take over as chairman and we instituted a search for a chief executive to replace him. At the same time David Newlands joined as a non-executive director. He had been finance director of GEC under Arnold Weinstock, with whom he had worked very closely, and had understandably decided to retire when his leader did. He was an excellent addition to the board.

Again it was another good year, with record profits before tax of £60 million, 20 per cent higher than in 1996, and net cash at the year end stood at £20 million. Altogether therefore it was a satisfactory moment at which to announce that I was standing down, although tempered for me by the realisation that I was the last of the founding family to be involved in the business. Four generations is probably quite enough, though, and in the view of some, perhaps it is more than enough. It was a great satisfaction, however, to be leaving the firm in such excellent hands, particularly those of Sir Ron Garrick and Ian Boyd. In their cases the worn phrase 'It was a privilege to work with them' had real meaning. Unlike some modern organisations, there was the bonus at Weir's of working with people who were good friends and kept their sense of humour, judgement and tolerance, however difficult the circumstances. What luck for anyone. In practice we did not take major decisions unless all three of us could agree. Sometimes perhaps Sir Ron and I might insist on something even if Ian Boyd disagreed, but that was seldom, and only when we thought he was erring on the conservative and cautious side. However, that is what the best Scottish accountants are surely expected to do.

An important event was that the consortium of Weir's, Balfour Beatty and Brown and Root finally became, after long, protracted and difficult negotiations, actual owners of Devonport rather than merely operators of the facility. The only sour note was that the Ministry of Defence insisted that Brown and Root become the majority shareholder. It cannot have been because there had been any problem in dealing with a consortium of these different shareholders (in any event by this time I was also chairman of Balfour Beatty) and we were sensible people. Rather it was a strange government belief that only Americans could run big projects. The fact that the US contractors based in the UK mainly employed British people, even at the top, seemed to be lost on them. At any rate they believed in some American mystique. For example, Bechtel were put in charge of sorting out not only the Channel Tunnel, but also the London Jubilee Line. Of course they did an excellent job in both, because they were experienced contractors who recognised that the common interest in a successful conclusion of a project was far more important than continuing some

sort of adversarial relationship between client and contractor – but not because they were American. Whatever the
reasoning of the Ministry of Defence (and indeed it is
sometimes a little difficult to identify 'reasoning' in the
mysterious workings of British government departments),
the management control of an important British defence
interest passed into foreign, albeit friendly, hands. Happily,
perhaps, the minister involved, although a delightful person,
is unlikely to hold public office again.

At the same time what was known as the D154 contract
was finally agreed. This contract covered the extensive
facilities for refitting and refuelling the nuclear submarine
fleet, a substantial part of which was also based at Devonport. The contract cost a great deal in the end, and in the
view of those closely involved much more than it reasonably should have done. Certainly it took far longer to finalise than it should have. If I were to say that excessive
attention was paid to the problems of nuclear safety, I would
naturally be accused of irresponsibility. The only comment
I will therefore make is simply to say that, although attention to detail and proper assessment of real risk must be
paramount, sometimes common sense is also quite useful,
and time is money.

One contract which was won that year is worth a
mention. A contract worth $20 million was awarded to the
Group by the World Bank to revamp the water supply at
Baku in Azerbaijan on the Caspian Sea. This was essential
to enable further development of the rich oil fields there.
The oil fields had originally been developed by the brother
of Alfred Nobel, the inventor of dynamite and ultimately
founder of the Nobel Prizes. Nobel was also an arms manufacturer and his brother had gone to that part of world
originally to look for hard wood to make rifle butts. The
younger brother developed the fields, and as a reward was

created Count Nobel by the Czar of Russia. Ultimately the
Nobels sold their interests to the Rothschilds in a piece of
excellent timing, given that the Russian Revolution was
not long to come. It was somewhat analogous to Lord
Cowdray's profitable sale of Mexican Eagle to Royal
Dutch/Shell in 1919, although it would be another twenty
years before oil in Mexico was nationalised by President
Lázaro Cárdenas. Due to the linguistic capabilities of Weir's
new employees in Salt Lake City, the company was able to
field an engineer who spoke Azeri, a rare talent.

The process of recruiting a new chief executive proved
a longer and more difficult one than expected. Location
was a distinct problem for some candidates from England.
One gentleman was delighted to come, provided the Group
headquarters moved to Oxfordshire. Simple parochialism
and the unwillingness of some wives to move very far from
their mothers were other factors. What a pathetic contrast
to the US attitude to moving as your career changes. My
own retirement was therefore postponed until January
1999. Duncan Whyte was appointed to be chief executive
from June 1999. He was an executive director of Scottish
Power with an excellent record in that electricity utility.
For the meantime it was agreed that Sir Ron would act as
both chairman and chief executive. Operating responsibility was divided between David Dunbar and Kevin Gamble,
with the former taking responsibility for pumps and service
activities and the latter for the other operations.

Again there was a record profit in 1998, of £71.6 million
before tax, although this did include an exceptional gain of
almost £8 million on the disposal of some peripheral businesses in South Africa and Australia. These had originally
been acquired as part of the purchase of EnviroTech, and
were now sold back to Baker Hughes, their original owner.

The stock market was weak, particularly in sectors such

as engineering. Perhaps it is not wholly unfair to observe that analysts often tend to take a view about whole sectors of the economy, rather than troubling themselves to see whether the prospects of individual companies are very different from those of the generality. Of course such folk endlessly ask for more information from companies. Intellectual idleness, or more likely the inclination not to move against fashion, seems to provide at times a strong disincentive to take an independent or indeed a logical view. They will say naturally that you cannot fight the sentiment of the market. They forget that lemmings say that before they dash over a cliff. The best investors – Warren Buffett, George Soros and Nils Taube, for example – take a different view. In any event, the Weir's share price looked disproportionately low, so the company bought in 4.25 million shares.

Two excellent acquisitions were made. The first of these, Entropie, had been founded by a relative of Jacob Rothschild and was introduced through the latter's good offices. It specialised in sophisticated heat exchange technology. For Weir's, the most interesting part of its business lay in thermo compression desalination, or TCD. In Weir Westgarth's flash distillation process, the source of energy to produce evaporation of the sea water is steam, usually as a by-product of power generation. A simplistic explanation of TCD is that the energy input is through recompressing, by means of a motor driven compressor, water vapour given off by the sea water. Weir's had many years previously built one or two such plants, in Gibraltar, for example, but they did not perform well. The vapour carried over from the sea water was not pure enough and contained an excessive salt content. The compressor used was a Howden Lysolm screw-compressor, which had very close tolerances between the inter-rotating screw elements, and was therefore subject to serious fouling problems when the salts precipitated on

the rotors. The Entropie plants used a much simpler compressor and were an excellent and reliable product which
could be well exploited commercially by Weir's market
position and reputation, especially in the Middle East.
Other products of Entropie were in some cases distinctly
esoteric. Vertical pig blood dryers were one. Another was an
extremely ingenious device to improve the all important
sugar concentration of grape juice in years which would
otherwise have produced a poor vintage in the wine trade.
I believe Pichon-Longueville was the first great chateau to
use their equipment, but still more notable houses (one
hesitates even to breathe their names) were quick to follow.
'So what?' one might say to this use of modern technology
in the great vineyards of Bordeaux. After all, many of them
already employ Australians as their wine makers.

The second acquisition was of Sebim S.A., a specialist
maker of safety valves, particularly for the power industry,
and therefore a very logical addition to a Group which
already included Hopkinson's. Sebim products were relay
operated safety valves of a sophisticated and highly effective
design. They were fitted to almost all of the French nuclear
power station programme. With the collapse of the Soviet
Union, and following the disaster of Chernobyl, there was
acute apprehension in the West, and most of all in Europe,
about the safety of nuclear stations in Russia and the former
Eastern Bloc. That was quite understandable, given that the
basic design of Chernobyl was one which had been rejected
as inherently too dangerous by both Britain and the USA
in the late 1940s, when they were considering the design
options for civil nuclear power. Indeed, the UK report of
the time stated (with scant regard to us Scots) that the only
place where a nuclear power station of that design could
reasonably be located in Great Britain was in the Western
Isles of Scotland. The European Union, as a neighbour, was

understandably anxious, and provided financial assistance to improve the safety of such reactors. Sebim benefited considerably from this programme, and continues to do so.

There were some interesting orders won during 1998. Weir Pumps was awarded an £18 million contract for diesel engine driven oil pipeline pumps for a major oil discovery made in the south of Sudan. The pipeline ran almost 1,000 miles to Port Sudan on the Red Sea. Given the severe political and religious problems in Southern Sudan, amounting in effect to civil war, the company received some criticism for being prepared to supply such equipment. In such cases, it always seems easier for political activists than for the manufacturer to make moral judgements with great certainty. Large orders were also won by Weir Pumps and the Group's valve companies for the Lungmen nuclear station in Taiwan and the Ling Ao station in China. Darchem had a particularly good year with strong demand from the aerospace and defence sectors. Profits before tax in 1998 were £71.6 million, including £7.9 million of exceptional items.

From some time before the acquisition of EnviroTech in 1994, Weir's had looked enviously at one Australian based business, Warman, which obviously fitted their criteria for acquisition. In 1999 this became a real possibility. Warman was a subsidiary of Peko Wallsend, a well known mining company. They were not interested in selling, for the simple and understandable reason that Warman made a steady and excellent profit contribution that clearly stabilised their overall earnings, which, as for all mining companies, were subject to the vagaries of metal prices. Some fundamental changes in the structure of the Australian mining sector, however, involving the need for capital to develop a major prospect, together with the intervention of North Broken Hill in the scene, led to Warman becoming available, and it operated in the same field as EnviroTech.

The ownership of EnviroTech obviously made Warman an even more attractive and logical purchase. In their internal analysis, Weir's expected savings from synergy to amount to some £8.3 million a year, and they expected to achieve about half of this in the first full year of amalgamation. Of course the proponents of mergers often talk loosely and wildly about the benefits of synergy. As we all know, however valid such calculations are, they never give any indication, in markets that become more and more competitive every year, of how much of the expected value of the savings has to be given away to customers simply to maintain the acquiring company's market position, and the modest residual amount which may actually benefit the shareholders themselves. As time went on, though, it was clear that in this case, through the provision of better service, improved technology and economies, the benefits to customers were as attractive to them as the improved returns were to shareholders. 'Win-win', as the idiotic phrase goes, was perhaps a reality for once.

Warman was therefore acquired late in 1999 for cash. It cost almost £190 million, and as a result net debt at year end was £146 million. This represented a gearing level of 57 per cent. When looking back at the very conservative comments about its finances which the Group had made for several years, the statement that this would improve the Group's financial structure seems a touch cynical, or at the least inconsistent. Actually, all that comment does is to highlight the fickle nature of financial fashion. Perhaps the closest analogy to the market's view of gearing is the question of whether skirts are too long or too short. The answer changes with the times, and I will neither go an inch further and reflect on whether bikini bathing suits are too large, nor make any improper comment, however tempting, about the current preoccupation in the business world with transparency.

The acquisition of Warman was of the greatest significance to the Group. The combination with the EnviroTech
business, carried out in exemplary fashion by David Dunbar,
produced a dominant force in the world mining market.
Particularly important in an industry where equipment is
obviously subject to the most arduous and wearing operational conditions, Weir's strong interest and commitment to
service was highly important. Not only was Weir's now in
a predominant position as pump suppliers to the industry,
but they also, through both Warman and EnviroTech, could
provide other vital and appropriate equipment such as
cyclones, valves, protected piping and the like, and even the
willingness to build service installations thousands of feet
up in locations like the Andes. I have commented already
on the loss of the commercial marine business – previously
a pillar of Weir's success over many years – but the entry
into the mining and metals industry through these acquisitions was a more than effective replacement for that loss. In
a short time the boom in basic commodities, both in
demand and in price, was happily to make this shift in
Weir's activities even more attractive. As in golf, you sometimes deserve what they call 'the rub of the green'.

Otherwise 1999 was not an easy year. There was a real
shortage of short-term orders, those that the company
called 'in-outs' (meaning orders due for delivery in the year
that they were booked). Longer term orders, however, were
well ahead of invoiced sales, giving some optimism for
future prospects. Profits before tax fell quite significantly,
mainly as a result of these short-term problems. As far as the
individual Group companies were concerned, Strachan and
Henshaw obtained major long-term contracts for the
nuclear submarine programme worth £57 million, and
£44 million of desalination work was won in the Middle
East. Darchem had a particularly good year, but the

activities of both Weir Pumps and Engineering Services were adversely affected by poor demand, both in the power market and in the North Sea. Hopkinson's also suffered a setback from the downturn in North Sea activity, which was particularly unwelcome as they had made strenuous and effective efforts in the preceding years to position themselves, both by new products and marketing initiatives, in the oil industry.

During the year there were changes to the board. As already related, Duncan Whyte had become chief executive in June. Bobby Bertram, who had been a stalwart non-executive director since 1982, retired. Two new non-executives were appointed. Christopher Clarke, previously with Shell, Samuel Montagu and the HongKong Shanghai Bank, and Jim Cox, previously with the investment side of Schroders and the Prudential (for a long time a supporter of the company), both joined during the year. At the same time Alan Mitchelson became company secretary, and Bill Harkness, who had filled the position with great competence, wisdom and distinction for 22 years, said he wished to retire during the following year as a director. Outsiders often do not understand how important the job of company secretary is. Companies themselves often used to be reluctant to reward these key individuals adequately. Their function today is becoming more and more important, particularly as they are not only the interface with growing (and often unjustified) regulatory and bureaucratic burdens, but also with the fashionable growth in litigation.

In 2000 there was a strong recovery of 28 per cent in operating profit, 15 per cent in pre-tax profits and 15 per cent in earnings per share from the somewhat disappointing results of 1999. Most importantly, net debt, which had increased substantially with the acquisition of Warman for borrowed cash, came down sharply by £51 million.

During the year Darchem was sold. After management changes which had been made in recent years it had certainly prospered, particularly with the help of a strong aviation market, and indeed it was by this stage earning record profits. Weir's considered, probably correctly, that to ensure its long term future in the aerospace industry, which was not Weir's main market, it either had to become significantly larger – and that could only be by acquisition – or else it should join another grouping. Weir's had more pressing priorities and Darchem was therefore sold to a management buyout. It had however certainly been a good purchase, and without doubt if the British nuclear programme had continued as expected at the time of its acquisition, it would have remained part of the Group.

The all-important integration of EnviroTech and Warman ran ahead of programme. In addition to the improved and wider product lines in the mining and metals industry which the Warman acquisition had brought to the Group overall, it also contributed (as EnviroTech had done through its Begemann operation) to a wider range of products in the hydrocarbon and chemical industries. Combined with Weir Pumps' existing activities, for the first time the Weir Group began to have the makings of a comprehensive product range to meet the overall demands of so important a group of customers.

In spite of the improved results overall, there were problems in some parts of the business. Hopkinson's had a difficult time, and their steel foundry was closed. Their soot-blower business was also sold. At Strachan and Henshaw it was decided to withdraw from their activities in the bulk handling of coal and minerals. They had certainly been successful in consistently winning important orders, but this seemed to be one of those curious businesses where, although there are not many competitors with the necessary technical competence, those involved seem to have an almost masochistic inclination to regard slim margins as a necessary and inevitable part of life. Quite rightly, therefore, Weir's decided to concentrate their efforts in the future on Strachan and Henshaw's business in the nuclear and defence fields.

During the year, apart from the retirement of Bill Harkness as a director, Howard Macdonald and Jack Urquhart also indicated their intention to retire. A company of Weir's size was very fortunate to have had two non-executive directors of their stature and experience for so long a period. Chris Fay joined the board, and clearly, as former chairman of Shell UK Limited, brought to the Group very relevant experience in a market so important to it.

In July, however, Duncan Whyte, who had been appointed as chief executive one year previously, resigned. In such circumstances, the natural and proper comment is that it is a regrettable and sad matter. In truth the fault, if there is one, lies almost always and almost entirely with those who appointed the individual concerned. This may not be the case when a person has served for a long time, but if matters do not work out in a short time frame, then it is those who have selected an individual who have made the largest part of an unfortunate judgement and choice. In the meantime, until a replacement was selected, Sir Ron continued in the joint role of chairman and chief executive, with David Dunbar in the role of chief operating officer.

In 2001, the operating results of the Group showed little change from the previous year. Some disposals of non-core operations were made. Weir Systems, after its earlier period of success, had run into difficulties, probably the result of inadequate management. Tooling Products and G. Perry, both heavily involved in the automobile industry, had also enjoyed a long period of satisfactory results after their initial acquisition by Weir's, but had more recently encountered considerable difficulty both from competition and from the state of their customer industry. All three were therefore sold.

The balance sheet of the Group improved once again. At year end, net debt was reduced to £66 million, representing quite modest gearing of 23 per cent and a great advance from the figure of £146 million only two years previously, which had resulted from the Warman acquisition. This progress certainly justified the decision to buy Warman for cash. Another initiative which was quite properly taken was to change the structure of the Group's debt, by switching much of the borrowing into liabilities denominated in Australian or US dollars, and thus automatically hedging currency exposure to the Group's now substantial assets in those countries.

A sour note on the financial scene was on the pensions front. In 1997, in one of the most hypocritical (and at the time far from adequately criticised) budget changes, Chancellor Gordon Brown, who had chanted the word 'prudence' like a soap powder advertisement, changed the rules for pension funds with regard to tax credits on dividends. Combined with a fall in stock markets and a decline in interest rates, this had a devastating effect on defined-benefit pension schemes. Lest my comment seems too anti-Labour and political, it is only fair to add that some years previously a Conservative Chancellor had ruled that if pension funds were, in the opaque view of the Treasury, over-funded, then they had to reduce this. This led to companies taking a 'contribution holiday', with the obvious eventual consequences. One supposes that in the minds of the wonderfully intelligent mandarins of the Treasury there lurked some suspicion that over-funded pension funds were some kind of subtle tax dodge, rather than a reflection of

either good investment management or a recognition that
a large surplus was a prudent and necessary nest-egg against
the certainty of volatile equity markets. Accordingly Weir's,
which had long had an admirable, prudent and successful
fund, was obliged, like so many other companies, to close
its defined benefit fund to new entrants. How quickly can
a self-righteous son of the manse, endowed with that certainty of the moral virtue of his own views (an attitude so
deplored by my ancestor, Robert Burns), contribute so
greatly to the destruction of the British system which had
previously been the best and most admired corporate
pension system in the West.

In 2001 and 2002 there were fundamental changes both
in the management of the Group and in the composition
of the board. Mark Selway, an Australian whose background
was in the automotive industry, became chief executive in
June 2001. David Dunbar retired in August, having made a
great contribution to the Group in a number of different
roles. Kevin Gamble resigned in November. Early in 2002
it was announced that Sir Robert Smith was to take over
from Sir Ron Garrick as chairman at the end of June. Sir
Robert had had a distinguished career at Deutsche Asset
Management, and brought to the Group his valuable con-
nections with the financial markets, together with wisdom,
business experience, and a strong commitment to matters
Scottish.

Sir Ron's retirement was a landmark in the history of
Weir's. He had worked with the firm for almost forty years.
He had been largely responsible for its recovery from 1981
onwards, and for the years of exceptional growth which
were then achieved. This he achieved through a combination of determination, intelligence and leadership. Unfairly
he was sometimes depicted as a little grim. A newspaper
article once unkindly said, 'He smiles at nine in the morning,

to get it over with for the day.' For those like Ian Boyd and myself who worked so closely with him for so long, the impression was quite different from that. It was a great pleasure to work with someone of such decency, friendliness and admirable character, and the best of Scots.

9

The past and the future

In the previous chapters I have given a highly personal view of the history of Weir's over the 130 years from its foundation up to 2002. In that year Sir Ron Garrick retired as chairman, to be succeeded by Sir Robert Smith (subsequently made a life peer), joining the new chief excutive, Mark Selway.

During that period the firm certainly experienced its share of mixed fortunes. From its foundation until the end of the First World War, it enjoyed almost continuous growth and high profitability. Between the wars, or at least until naval rearmament began in 1936, there was a period of great difficulty, with shipbuilding, the company's major market, being particularly hard hit by the worldwide depression. There followed another period of growth and prosperity lasting until the early 1960s, during which the real problem was in meeting demand rather than winning orders. Thereafter there were difficult times during the 1970s when, although important foundations were laid for the future through acquisitions, the dilemma of simultaneously trying to reduce the company's level of debt while keeping up the momentum of growth could not be resolved, culminating, when trading conditions turned down, in the crisis of 1980 that led to capital reconstruction.

From 1983 the firm's fortunes changed dramatically for the better, and exceptionally strong growth ensued for ten years or so. The final ten years up to 2002 were highly important. Although steady growth in profits faltered somewhat towards the end of this period, the acquisitions of Warman and EnviroTech were as important as anything the Group had ever done. These acquisitions gave a size and spread, in both geography and products, to the pump business – and to the closely related activity in valves – and thus provided the opportunity to operate for the first time as a real force worldwide. That is the legacy which the management of today have inherited.

They have also inherited challenges, and it is worth considering how well Weir's is positioned, in its current form, to meet some of the more obvious of these, such as globalisation and the emerging economies; diversification and risk; investor expectations; and maintaining independence.

Ron Garrick's retirement and the appointment of Sir Robert Smith and Mark Selway as chairman and chief executive mark a significant stage in Weir's development, and before looking at the challenges facing the Group, it is therefore necessary to give some account of changes in policy and direction as well as of progress from that point.

In 2001 a strategic review was carried out by Mark Selway, the main conclusions of which were that long-term success could best be achieved through a radical programme, which it was envisaged would take some five years to complete. In summary, this programme comprised: increasing competitiveness through better productivity and a strong emphasis on lean manufacture as pioneered in the automotive industry; investing in those areas which had the best return in a short period, and simplification of the overall business by disposals; attacking new markets and searching for acquisitions which fitted the company's structure; and preserving or improving market share and margins by new product development.

To these ends the business was initially reorganised into five product groups on a global basis. These were as follows:

- Slurry: this covered mineral processing. Happily it was later renamed 'Minerals', thus removing the connotation with odiferous farmyard waste products.
- Clear Liquids: mainly covering the oil, power, and water industries, and including such individual operating units as Weir Pumps at Cathcart.
- Valves and Controls: including the operations of Hopkinson's in the UK, Atwood and Morrill in the USA, and Sebim in France.
- Engineering Services.
- Contracting: this group was subsequently renamed 'Techna' and included desalination, liquid gas handling and storage, and the nuclear and submarine weapons activities of Strachan and Henshaw.

In parallel, widespread changes were made in senior management. Training, succession planning and employee appraisal were put on to a more formal and organised basis, and the system of rewarding management for good performance was refined. From the start, the main emphasis was on pumps and valves as manufactured products, and a start was made on increasing the focus on such activities by the disposal of some non-core activities. As a result, Weir Systems, Tooling Products and G. Perry were all sold during 2001, resulting in a provision of £14.9 million.

The results for 2001 were a pretax profit, excluding amortisation of goodwill and exceptional items, of £60 million on sales of £900 million. It was a difficult year for the clear liquids business and Hopkinson's, but a good one for LGE, engineering services, desalination and valve operations in the USA. Alan Mitchelson was appointed director responsible for corporate services, in addition to being company secretary.

In 2002, further steps towards rationalising the structure of the company were taken through the disposal of the shareholding in First Engineering, the rail maintenance company. The timing was fortuitous, as shortly afterwards conditions in the rail industry became confused and difficult, and an excellent profit was made on this investment. The Neyrfor oil drilling operation was also sold. With hindsight, given the subsequent strong rise in oil and gas prices and resulting boom in exploration, this was perhaps a decision of less clear-cut benefit. At the same time, pump manufacture by Girdlestone at Ipswich was transferred to Cathcart, and the Hazleton foundry in the USA was closed.

Profits were virtually unchanged, with the minerals business and engineering services performing particularly well. A feature of the year was the dramatic improvement in the balance sheet, driven by disposals and good operating cash flow, and resulting in a modest net cash position compared with £68 million debt at the previous year end.

Pretax profit for 2003 was slightly lower at £57 million, but again there was a good cash flow from operations at £56 million. Clear Liquids improved, and Minerals had a good year, with orders from China and Russia and a strong performance in South America. Engineering Services had an excellent year, with operating profits up by 33 per cent, and very good results both at Peacock in Canada and from refurbishing hydro-electric plant. The Techna division had lower profits and turnover, although new orders were excellent at £100 million, and included successes in sulphate removal plants for the offshore industry. The latter were installations to treat sea water so that it became inert and could be injected into oil wells without the danger of forming deposits of calcium sulphate scale, which would block the flow of oil. Chris Rickard joined as finance director to replace Ian Boyd on his retirement, and Michael Dearden, formerly with Castrol, became a non-executive director, while David Newlands and Chris Fay retired.

Profits were largely unchanged in 2004. The Minerals division again enjoyed an excellent year, which included sales of equipment for the Alberta tar sands, and their orders were up by 20 per cent. A new plant was opened by them in India at Bangalore. Engineering Services won an important contract to support the operations of BP and its partners in Azerbaijan. In the Techna division, further sulphate treatment orders were won, and LGE obtained the contracts for all the liquid gas ships ordered worldwide that year, a notable achievement. Stephen King from De la Rue and Lord Robertson of Port Ellen, previously Secretary General of NATO, joined the board as non-executive directors.

The most important developments were at Hopkinson's and in the Clear Liquids business, particularly at Cathcart. The unsatisfactory cost basis, excess space and awkward layout at Hopkinson's Huddersfield site was addressed by the decision to sell the site and move operations to a modern and more appropriately sized facility nearby, and this was carried out in the following year. In Clear Liquids, it was recognised that consolidation in the industry was not going to be achieved, and accordingly the product line was downsized by dropping less profitable lines and rationalising facilities with the implication that, as had been done at

Hopkinson's, the sale of the Cathcart site would be explored, together with relocation to a modern and smaller new facility. It was announced that these actions would require a provision of £31 million.

Pretax profits in 2005 improved somewhat to £62 million. The balance sheet now however included £76 million in debt, compared with £12 million cash at the previous year end. This reflected some of the costs of restructuring, together with a contribution of £10 million to the pension fund and the purchase of the Gabbioneta pump business in Italy. This firm mainly served the downstream oil industry and was an important acquisition in strengthening the product line of the Clear Liquids operation, particularly in the hydro-carbons industries.

The Minerals division had another excellent year, particularly in South America. Two examples were pumps supplied for iron ore pipelines in Brazil and for flue gas desulphurisation plant in China. LGE had another record year, booking £80 million in orders. Incidentally, the demand for transportation and storage facilities for liquid petroleum gases such as butane and propane is driven to a large extent by the strong growth in natural gas, or LNG, liquifaction, where these gases are often a valuable by-product.

A major event during the year was the sale of the desalination activities. This marked something of a milestone, as desalination had been pioneered by Weir's, first by James Weir himself in the nineteenth century and then by the development of the modern multi-flash system in the late 1950s. The rationale for disposing of it was that margins were low and major plants were now on such a large scale that the value of such contracts itself not only represented a significant financial risk, but also required very large bonding facilities. Moreover the timing of awards for major plants had always been very erratic, varying between more work than could easily be handled and a complete dearth at times. Clearly if a company wanted to show any steady growth, such an activity could have a very distorting effect. Set against that, little working capital was required in most cases, and risk could be offset to a considerable degree by 'pay when paid' arrangements with major suppliers.

Three other important developments must be noted: the establishment of a valve plant in China; increased local presence there by the Minerals division; and the decision to move the head office of the Weir Group from Cathcart, where it had long been a tenant of Weir Pumps, to independent offices in downtown Glasgow. Such a move had been seriously considered once before, in the mid 1960s, even to the extent that an option had been taken on a building and architect's plans made, but it had then been dropped.

The goals which the 2001 Strategic Review had set were obviously ambitious and demanding. Nor were the initiatives involved generally such as could achieve their objectives and produce positive improvements to the Group's results in any very short timescale. Some did produce early results, however. For example, the time from concept to market for new products improved both quickly and dramatically, as did economies in working capital. Naturally the benefits were bound to be offset by the disruption which inevitably accompanies any radical change, and by the initial cost burden of starting up new activities and of relocation and changing factory layouts. Given the extent of change, the Group results in the period from 2001 were very reasonable indeed. Profits, before tax and exceptional items, ran steadily at around the £60 million per annum mark. Cash generated from operations was remarkably consistent for four out of five years at around £70 million a year.

The measure of success or failure of the five-year plan

would clearly be the results for 2006. In the event, these results were most encouraging. Profits before tax, excluding exceptional items, increased by 40 per cent to £87 million for the continuing operations of the Group. Order input at £1,099 million showed a 23 per cent increase, cash generation was £134 million, and the year ended with net debt of a mere £7 million. It would be difficult to see these results as anything but a strong vindication of the strategy and programme set in 2001 by Mark Selway. During the year, Keith Cochrane took over as finance director.

It can of course be argued – perhaps ungenerously – that in key markets, particularly minerals and oil, demand has been excellent. That has certainly been the case. I would suggest however that only the most obdurate of pessimists would foresee a major setback in these markets in the near future. The demand for minerals is driven by the Chinese economy. Moreover, given the brutal service conditions to which mining equipment is subjected, spares and service demand is disproportionate in that industry and should certainly continue at a strong and profitable level. In the oil and gas industry, even if the present elevated price levels reduce, the decline in production of existing fields together with a shortage of refinery capacity must continue to stimulate investment strongly. Furthermore, the increased politicisation of oil and gas supplies by Russia and instability in the Middle East must continue to support the importance of developing new resources elsewhere. In power, key markets such as China and India will have shortages of capacity even if their rate of growth in demand were to fall, and in that market there is in any event the strong possibility of a resurgence in the nuclear generation field. In addition, as has already been said, the demand for transportation and storage of LPG is certain to grow as more liquid natural gas facilities are put in place.

Early in 2007 an announcement was made which in terms of the firm's history was dramatic indeed. Some time earlier it had been made public that the Group was considering the sale of the Cathcart site and relocation to a new and more appropriately sized site in the area. What emerged, however, was a quite different outcome. The Group entered into negotiations to sell the clear liquid business of Weir Pumps to Sulzer in Switzerland. (This business basically consisted of pump activities in the power station and upstream oil industry, the products for these markets including such equipment as boiler feed pumps, oil pipeline pumps and oilfield injection pumps.)

For ten years it had been clear to Weir's, and indeed to Sulzer, that amalgamation, in one form or other, of their two businesses in these sectors would generate significant benefits. Products of this type require not only substantial design and engineering effort, but also major investment in heavy specialised machine tools and, above all, very expensive test facilities, particularly for nuclear reactor and boiler feed pumps. Competition, moreover, not simply between these two firms but with others, had led to poor margins, which in Weir's case were well below those earned in the rest of its pump business. At one point Weir's had attempted to buy Sulzer's business, without success. Their decision now to sell was strongly influenced by changes in the Chinese power station market, which had become much the most important one, and where the authorities had decided – not unreasonably – on much more equipment, such as pumps, being locally sourced. Sulzer was already established in China, including having a major test facility there, and Weir's were not. Sulzer's domestic test facility in the UK was moreover also a modern one. The alternative for Weir's was therefore to try to catch up, and not only would this have taken considerable time, but it would also have involved a very large investment.

In the event, the proposed sale to Sulzer fell through, but shortly after negotiations broke down, the company was instead sold for some £48 million to Jim McColl, a former Weir's apprentice, who had built up a highly successful international engineering group based originally on the modest Glasgow firm of Clyde Blowers. He announced that the business would operate under the name of Clyde Pumps Ltd, and that he would proceed with the original Weir's plan of moving to a modern new plant, to be built nearby when the Cathcart site was vacated for proposed housing development in 2009. Weir's would continue to provide service facilities to Clyde Pumps in a number of areas and to supply them with special materials from the foundry in Manchester.

Even after disposing of this part of the product line, however, the Group will still retain a considerable exposure to the oil and power markets. They have a growing presence in the downstream oil industry, such as refinery and petrochemical pumps. In power they have a strong position in flue gas desulphurisation, an important area. And in both markets they have an excellent product line in high quality valves for conventional and nuclear power plant and oil industry service. To put the whole exercise in perspective, the sale covered less than 8 per cent of Group turnover and less than 5 per cent of profits.

These developments cannot, however, be looked at simply in economic or business terms. In the history of Weir's, they also truly represent a huge break with the past. The business was founded originally to exploit three technologies: boiler feed pumps; heat exchange through condensing plant and the closed feed system; and desalination through the sea water evaporator. For well over a hundred years, these were the core of the business and the products for which it was famous. Heat exchange was the first to disappear, mainly as a result of the consolidation of the heavy power plant business, first under GEC in Britain and Alsthom in France and then the amalgamation of those two, which left little or no place for an independent supplier like Weir's. Desalination, as has already been recounted, was sold because it had become essentially a large-scale contracting business, rather than a manufactured product, and its scale and risk did not fit easily with the rest of Weir's activities. The main market in the Middle East was moreover one where low price rather than value had become the chief consideration. The rationale behind the disposal or closure of the part of the clear liquid product range which included boiler feed and nuclear pumps has already been explained. While not quarrelling with that rationale, it is however worth commenting that equipment of that type is technically among the most demanding parts of the pump industry, and there is perhaps a danger to the longer term level of technical expertise in the Group if it is no longer exposed to meeting some of the difficult technical challenges such products involve, particularly in such areas as reliability and hydraulic efficiency. Doubtless, however, there are plenty of other technical challenges in the pump industry, as doubtless there is also a strong recognition of the vital importance of maintaining technical excellence.

The decision to sell the Cathcart site prompts other reactions. For those who worked there, there were the obvious uncertainties and painful difficulties which a closure of such a kind involves, even though the new owner indicated that there would be no redundancies. For the much larger number, now mainly retired, who once worked there, many of them for all their working lives, it is something different and a matter of real sadness and loss. For the local community it is the disappearance of a landmark so long established as to be part of Glasgow's history. Indeed for many people the firm has not simply been Weir's, but Weir's of Cathcart. Such feelings are understandable and cannot just be dismissed as sentiment. After all, Cathcart was not just one factory – and recently not even the largest in a company which has some twenty manufacturing plants around the world – but it was also the location of the Group's headquarters for over 130 years. The fact that the Group's headquarters remain in Glasgow, and that it still remains the last major engineering manufacturer to be run from Scotland, will not perhaps be much compensation to such people.

It must however be said that having both a major manufacturing centre of the Group and the Group's headquarters in one location had not in earlier days been without serious difficulties. As already recounted, there had been substantial problems with internal politics in Kenneth Weir's time as chairman, and these had caused, at an early and crucial stage, considerable difficulty in establishing a rational structure for the group business. These problems were caused by turf wars mainly between what might be called the Cathcart executive establishment and the rest. The Cathcart establishment not only wanted to continue running the major single part of the Group, but certainly wished to continue their primary position above all others. In practical terms this meant they wanted priority for their views, specifically in terms of their ideas for expansion, diversification or investment. The chairman's role, as has been said earlier, was clearly very difficult at that time, and had it not been for the friction and politics caused by the 'Cathcart factor', then an effective and rationally based group structure could have been put in place much sooner, to obvious benefit.

Today's developments need to be viewed not with regret or sentiment, however, but in a much wider context. The business world has changed most dramatically in a very short period – certainly very rapidly in comparison with previous times. The Weir Group for some time has been a global enterprise rather than a Scottish manufacturer. Change requires change – although some of the more cynical of us may still secretly admire the splendid and all too often true saying, 'All change is for the worse.'

Clearly the agreements to sell Weir Pumps would produce a transformation of the financial position of the Group, bringing in £45 million for the business, excluding the value of the site itself. Added to this was the announcement in May 2007 of the sale of the Group's shareholding in Devonport dockyard to Babcock for a cash consideration of approximately £85 million. Taken together with the bank facilities available to the Group and its continuing strong cash flow, it was now obviously possible to make a major acquisition or acquisitions. Indeed it was highly desirable to do so, not only to replace the turnover and profits of the operations disposed of, but ideally also to produce a new direction for growth complementary to the existing business of the Group. This is exactly what was achieved by the announcement in June 2007 of the acquisition of SPM Flow Control Inc., the Texas based manufacturer of well-service pumps and associated flow control products, key equipment in the upstream sector of the oil and gas industry. SPM's pumps, which form the largest part of their product line, are used particularly in gas fields for such duties as cementing wells and fracturing to enhance production flows. Financially this is much the largest acquisition ever made by Weir's, at a purchase price of some $653 million. The company is the leader in its field, with an overall 48 per cent market share, sales of $323 million and pre-tax profits of $56 million in 2006. Not only has this acquisition greatly increased Weir's involvement in the excellent continuing prospects of the oil and gas industry, but there also appear to be good opportunities for improving the costs and efficiency of an already profitable concern. Altogether it is an excellent fit with Weir's other activities.

A further important acquisition announced at the end of 2007 and completed in March 2008 was that of the C. H. Warman Pump Group, which supplies specialist pumps for the mining and minerals industries in Africa. Some years previously, Weir's had acquired Warman International, which had a common parenthood to C. H. Warman, and a similar product line. It was based in Australia and covered worldwide markets outside Africa, and today trades as Weir Warman. C. H. Warman is a profitable business with its head office and main factory in Johannesburg, and it employs some 430 people. Quite obviously it is an acquisition which fits in very neatly with Weir's other activities in this field, and which will further strengthen the company.

The results for 2007 were a further strong justification of the policies and plans set out in 2002. Turnover exceeded £1 billion for the first time, and profits before tax were £120 million. Operating cash flow was strong, and the order book at year end was over £1 billion.

In summary, therefore, the series of major developments from 2002, after Mark Selway became chief executive, up to 2008 would seem to have set the Weir Group up very satisfactorily, so that the markets in which they were most engaged and where their relative position was strongest were also those with good prospects for continuing prosperity in the long term. At the same time a further change in the structure of the Group was announced in 2008. It was now reconstituted as three divisions: Mining and Minerals, Oil and Gas, and Power and Industrial, under the management of Scot Smith, Stephen Bird and Phil Clifton respectively. Service activities fell into the individual divisions as appropriate. Apart from the organisational benefits, this made clear just where the activities of the Group were now focused.

At the beginning of that period, the company's production systems and their performance were below acceptable industry standards. For example, on-time delivery of pumps was running at only 47 per cent. Today it is over 90 per cent. There were several loss-making companies, and some businesses were certainly non-core. Product and material development and investment in information technology systems were not what they should have been. In commercial terms, geographic coverage was incomplete. Above all, margins and cash generation needed to improve substantially. The energetic action taken during the period has produced radical improvement in all these areas. Above all, the clearest indication of success is that the share price tripled over those five years.

It has been a very successful period in Weir's history, with the market capitalisation touching £2 billion and the company on the threshold of joining the FTSE100 list of leading UK public companies – a terrific transformation under Lord Smith and Mark Selway.

This chapter started by setting out not only the legacy which the management of the Group today inherited, but also some of the challenges. One of these was globalisation, and that has been the largest single force for change. This is therefore the first context in which we should judge the radical changes the Group has made. Indeed, if the Group's reactions have been either inadequate or inappropriate, then this would be a real cause for concern. Globalisation has been caused by the emergence, largely simultaneously, of a number of interrelated factors which include liberalisation of trade; freer movement of capital (due to the abolition of many exchange control regimes); radical improvements in the cost and speed of transportation, mainly resulting from the development of container shipping; and changes in the economic and political situation in a number of countries and regions. Obviously the prime examples of the latter are China and India. China has discarded the crazy policies of Chairman Mao's communist regime. India has, to a degree at least, started to free itself from the stifling combination of bureaucracy, socialism and misguided nationalism which were the impoverishing legacy of the Nehru clan. In addition, South Korea and parts of South East Asia have for long been part of the modern business world, and in the Americas the formation of NAFTA has been another contributing factor. I suspect that Adam Smith might with good reason have viewed globalisation simply as a logical extension of the Industrial Revolution.

A further influence has been the development of the logistics industry on a large scale. Whether all these various elements are the result of globalisation or contributors to it is as pointless a question as that about the chicken and the egg.

The combination of these factors has had many beneficial results. World trade has grown at a much faster rate than world output. The speed of progress in the developing countries has made them into strong markets for capital goods and raw materials. On the supply side, the abundant cheap labour in those countries has turned them into efficient low cost producers. In the West, and particularly in the USA, easy credit policies and cheap money have, at least until 2008, supported consumer demand, albeit with unfavourable and perhaps unsustainable effects on both the balance of payments and on saving. The supply chain for both the consumer and the producer in the West has simultaneously been revolutionised.

The international challenge of globalisation to any British company like Weir's has been reinforced by the steady process of de-industrialisation of the UK economy. In the earliest days of the company, the domestic market, particularly in shipbuilding, had a size and growth which could sustain an expanding business, and particularly one which developed new products to meet new demands. Even after the Second World War, although export markets were important, domestic demand for capital goods remained strong, and the shortage of manufacturing capacity permitted high profit margins for a period of some fifteen years.

In today's world of globalisation, success requires a combination of three initiatives. Advantage must be taken of the cheaper sourcing available; products, where possible, should be developed which by their nature and technology provide difficult entry barriers for potential competitors, and thus can both enjoy good margins and remain suitable for export; and the marketing and manufacturing battle must be carried geographically into customer territory overseas. On these grounds it would seem that the Group is well placed.

Another future challenge any company must face is that of diversification and risk. As far as diversification goes, I believe that Weir's is well placed. To the casual observer, pump manufacture may appear to be a single specific activity. Fortunately pumps, and indeed valves, are needed in so wide a range of industries and applications that they inherently offer an automatic diversification. Moreover, although the markets and applications are so varied, there is a good degree of commonality in the basic design technology and in the manufacturing facilities required.

As for risk, Weir's position today is distinctly better than in the past. The Group has now withdrawn from desalination, and some years earlier, for reasons already described, also discontinued its involvement in heat exchange. For many years, at least until 1960, this equipment could be manufactured in the shops at Cathcart. Latterly the invention of multiple flash desalination plants, and the consequent great increase in their size, together with their construction as large steel fabrications, made their continuing manufacture in Weir's facilities impractical. Desalination became in effect a contract engineering activity, with the amount of supply by Weir's itself hardly amounting to 10 per cent of the contract value. Moreover the value of the contracts for desalination grew rapidly, in some cases exceeding £100 million. Margins in such contracting are not high. Kenneth Weir used to say, albeit in the context of civil contracting, that 'Three per cent is satisfactory, five per cent is good, and if you make seven per cent you are called Bechtel.' There were indeed years where desalination profits made an important contribution to the Group's results. There were also disasters, such as the Bahamas contract in the late 1950s, and in the 1980s the Ad Dur reverse-osmosis contract in Bahrain wiped out the profits made by desalination over many other years, even if its effect on the overall results of the Group was happily disguised from the outside world by the strong performance of the rest of the business. In addition, obtaining due payments was not always easy in some Middle East markets, and the irregularity of contracts added volatility to the Group's overall results.

In summary, therefore, both in terms of diversification and risk, Weir's current concentration on its pump and valve activities appear to place it in a good position to face the future. Certainly those investors who attach importance to the fashionable concept of 'focus' can surely have no cause for complaint.

It now seems clear that there will be a strong revival

worldwide in nuclear power, after a long period when new construction was dormant (except in the Far East), due to public perceptions, or perhaps misconceptions, shaped variously by the disasters at Three Mile Island in the USA and Chernobyl in Russia, by the bad-mouthing of the nuclear industry by environmentalists, and above all by cowardly political leadership in the democracies. A major opportunity and challenge will therefore be posed by this renaissance. Weir's in the past had a heavy involvement in nuclear power, particularly through Weir Pumps and Strachan and Henshaw. The disposal of Weir Pumps and the announcement of the sale of Strachan and Henshaw in 2008 clearly much reduces the Group's exposure to the industry, but all of its valve operations are well established as major suppliers of key nuclear equipment, so there should be some considerable compensation here.

Another challenge is to maintain technical leadership and innovation. Fundamental inventions affecting pump or valve equipment are difficult to envisage today. Advance is now much more a question of incremental improvement and often of superior application engineering. It is at least as difficult, if not more so, to obtain an improvement of a small percentage in the efficiency of centrifugal pumps as it was to invent the whole concept in the first place. That is not to say that radical innovation is not possible. The two-phase pump for the oil industry was one radical concept, and there are and will be others. There are other examples of unusual and interesting (and even amusing!) developments by Weir's. Pumps that can propel migrating salmon, of large size, up past high hydro-electric dams, with a survival rate of almost 100 per cent, are just one. (Incidentally, on arrival at the top of the dam after this unusual and unnatural journey some of the salmon were apparently tested for stress, journey-induced, I suppose, like in the case

of British Airways passengers, and happily they passed such
a test. Quite how you assess a salmon for stress is a mystery
to me. On rivers where they operate 'catch and release' I
have always found the salmon quite enthusiastic when you
let them go.) Weir's equipment has also pumped large
quantities of tomatoes over distance without damage. Given
that the average supermarket tomato is quite like a cricket
ball in hardness, colour and taste, that may say as much
about the nature of the tomatoes as it does about the pump
maker's art. Overall, however, there is no reason to think
that Weir's will fall behind in the technical challenge, and
certainly the management clearly appears to have no intention that it will.

Another challenge for Weir's, as it has always been for
publicly quoted companies, is to meet investor expectations. It might of course be observed, without undue cyni-
cism, that the first difficulty in meeting expectations is to
establish what those expectations actually are, let alone
what they might be in the longer term. Since Weir's became
a public company some sixty years ago, not only have the
investor's expectations changed, but so has his identity. The
individual private investor has long since ceased to be a
very significant force in the market . His involvement today
is largely an indirect one through life assurance, pensions,
investment funds and other financial vehicles, and it is not
the expectations of numerous individuals which need to be
met, but the expectations of those who manage funds on
their behalf.

The attitude of these institutional investors has also
changed in recent times. Until perhaps 25 years ago, institutions like the great insurance companies were, on the whole,
long term holders in the firms in which they invested. The
Prudential, for example, for a long period held around 5
per cent of the shares in most leading British companies.

They kept in good touch with managements, whom they encouraged to maintain a frank dialogue with them. Equally they would certainly say something to a company if things were going awry, and their observations were not lightly disregarded. This sort of relationship, which had much to commend it, became impossible when those who regulated the stock market decreed in their wisdom that if a company gave information to one shareholder it had to do so to all. This was done in the name of fair competition and that vague concept called transparency, but it also indirectly implied that if a company had confidential discussions with just one shareholder, that shareholder might abuse the confidence and take advantage of it. It is hard to think of anything that would have been further from the character of such past investment managers of the Prudential as the celebrated Messrs Murray and Moody.

The relationship between a company and its major institutional shareholders therefore changed from private discussion to the typical analyst conferences of today. It is perhaps unlikely that this really makes it easier to know what investor expectations are.

At the same time, institutional investors, particularly those who manage pension funds, have also changed their behaviour. Clients not only regularly review the performance of the fund managers – and that is right and proper – but many of them judge that performance on a short-term basis, which is quite another matter, and change managers accordingly. Although competition is in general healthy and commendable, it is unlikely that this practice actually produces better investment returns. What it does however mean for public companies is that their short-term performance is increasingly scrutinised and acted upon by investors, even when the nature of their business is cyclical or long term. Moreover there is today a substantial volume of investment which has not the slightest interest in the long-term prospects of a company, or in the dividend it pays, or sometimes even in what it does, but only in the short-term movement in its share price and the possibility of it being taken over. In the case of hedge funds, a share price moving down is at times just as interesting and remunerative as one moving up. Some people would comment that the shares in companies are today often more like chips in a poker game than a shared part in their prospects for the delivery of performance and prosperity.

Dividend policy is another matter of investor expectations. Its importance cannot be judged in absolute terms, since its significance varies from one class of investor to another. The market's view of its relative importance also changes from time to time. In Weir's case, the dividends paid have increased every year during the more than 25 years since the capital reconstruction. Measuring total return by a combination of dividend and share price movement is fashionable today, and during that period (which admittedly had an artificially low starting point) dividends have risen by a factor of roughly 11 times, and the share price by over 60 times. It is therefore unlikely that investors, or at least rational longer-term ones, should have cause for complaint, even if future progress were to be at a rather more modest pace.

A further consideration is what might perhaps be described as steadiness of progress. Certainly in an ideal world this is something which appeals to many investors, and implies a continuous year-by-year upward progression in earnings. On the positive side the exit from desalination, with its very large and long term contracts which only took place at irregular intervals, must help to smooth Weir's results.

Looked at overall, therefore, there is no case to be made

that Weir's does not or will not meet the reasonable expectations of reasonable investors, at least so far as those expectations can be defined. It is another question, however, as to whether that amounts to enough to keep the company independent.

Earlier in this history, I pointed out how many of the great names in Scottish engineering and allied industries had now disappeared and that Weir's was almost the sole survivor. On the wider British scene the picture is no different. The 'Engineering/Industrial' section in the stock-market pages of my newspaper shows only some two dozen companies which could reasonably be described as being in engineering, and only eleven of these are in the FTSE 250 list. Yet it is not so many years ago that engineering was one of the largest categories listed. Compare this situation with that in Germany, where a strength of their economy still remains the large number of privately owned specialist engineering companies, often international leaders in their fields. In Britain there are few of this kind. In spite of this rather bleak background, however, I do not think that it is by any means inevitable that Weir's will cease to be independent. Of course today there is a strong merger and acquisition culture, driven, as much as by anything, by the profits such transactions generate for the investment banks and their senior personnel. Indeed you are hard pressed today if you are considering making an acquisition to find an investment bank who will advise you not to do it, even though all bankers must be aware of the well publicised research which shows that most acquisitions do not create value.

Weir's strategy of divesting themselves of non-core businesses and concentrating on pumps and valves, quite apart from its business justification, should also reduce its attractiveness as an acquisition target. This is because there are no longer the opportunities for an acquirer to break up the company and recoup a substantial part of the acquisition cost by disposing of parts of it not central to its main opera-tions. Weir's have already done just that for themselves. Nor is the Group likely to become financially attractive because of surplus cash, as it is investing strongly, and is likely to continue to do so, given the investment opportunities avail-able to it. It has also clearly indicated its willingness to buy back its shares, and has already done so when the share price has been at a suitable level.

Weir's future will however depend in the end on the competence, skill and success of its management, as well as their confidence and their will to remain independent. It is important that they do remain independent. There are good reasons for this. Independent businesses are, for obvious social reasons, important to the communities in which they are established. More important than that is the clear identity which they have, and which they lend to those who work in them. To use an analogy from the armed forces, a soldier identifies with and feels he belongs to his regiment far more than he identifies with the infantry or the army in general, and so it is with the sailor and his ship. A firm is much stronger if those who work in it can iden-tify themselves with it and its purpose and values, and have a loyalty to it, rather than simply working for their pay cheque. It is much more difficult to achieve this state of affairs, which is important to many people in contributing to their stability and satisfaction from life, in huge organisa-tions with very large facilities or where the unit in which they work has no real identity and ethos of its own. As an extreme example, in a huge factory of a communist regime this situation is impossible to approach. Weir's have quite rightly avoided calling each company simply Weir, instead usually linking the Weir name with the previous name of the operation whenever the latter has an established identity of its own. In this way you have the best of both worlds – on the one hand the image of a strong international organisation, and on the other hand the important sense of local identity.

Far too many independent businesses have been lost to Scotland, and far too few of any significance have been created in recent years. There is a proud history behind Weir's, with plenty of examples of what to do and quite a few of what not to do. Let us hope that the old firm continues for many years to come. In the last few years Sir Robert Smith and Mark Selway have shown what a combination of traditional Scots virtues and the refreshing competitive outlook of an Australian can do. Certainly the business is in good hands.

In a little over sixty years from now, it will be time to mark the bicentenary of Weir's. It would be fascinating to know what the coming decades hold for the company. Perhaps there will be a further history of Weir's written at that time – how very satisfactory that would be.

Appendix:
Chairmen and key directors

This is a selective list of key figures. Dates have been provided for the chairmen only, but all names appear in chronological order of appointment.

Chairmen
James Weir
William, 1st Lord Weir: 1946–55★
Kenneth, 2nd Lord Weir: 1955–72★
William, 3rd Lord Weir: 1972–81★
Sir Francis (later Lord) Tombs: 1981–3
William, 3rd Lord Weir: 1983–99★
Sir Ronald Garrick: 1999–2002★
Sir Robert (later Lord) Smith: 2002–

Deputy or vice chairmen
Sir John Richmond★
James G. Weir
J. W. Drysdale
J. R. Lang★
S. L. Finch
★ = *also served at one time as either managing director or chief executive*

Chief executives or managing directors
C. R. Lang
Sir Ronald Garrick
Duncan Whyte
Mark Selway

Other senior directors or executives
Finance
J. Spittal
J. J. B. Young
E. D. Bremner
I. M. Boyd
Chris Rickard
Keith Cochrane

Technical
H. Hillier
R. S. Silver
G. F. Arkless
Hon. G. A. Weir

Housing
A. Cargill

Engineering
J. W. Atwell

Aircraft Equipment
C. F. Taylor
N. M. Niven

Foundries
S. L. Finch
A. Brearley

J. Ferguson

Water
A. C. Smith
P. B. Simpkin
P. Capell

International
J. de Raemy

Clear Liquids
Stephen Bird

Valves and Controls
Phil Clifton

Engineering Services
Peter Syme
Steve Simone

Mining and Minerals
Scot Smith

Oil and Gas
Stephen Bird

Power and Industrial
Phil Clifton

Company secretaries
J. Davidson
F. R. Frame
W. Harkness
A. Mitchelson

Index